W9-BUA-754

FRITZ WETHERBEE'S
NEW HAMPSHIRE

Fritz Wetherbee's
NEW HAMPSHIRE

Fritz Wetherbee

PLAIDSWEDE PUBLISHING
Concord, New Hampshire

Copyright © 2005, by Fritz Wetherbee

All rights reserved. No part of this work may be used or reproduced in any manner whatsoever without written permission from the publisher, except in the case of brief quotations embodied in critical articles and reviews.

ISBN-13: 978-0-9755216-5-6
ISBN-10: 0-9755216-5-9
Library of Congress Control Number: 2005933176

Designed and composed in Minion Pro
at Hobblebush Books,
Brookline, New Hampshire (www.hobblebush.com)
Printed in the United States of America

Published by:

PLAIDSWEDE PUBLISHING
P.O. Box 269 · Concord, New Hampshire 03302-0269
www.plaidswede.com

CONTENTS

THE TOWNS

THE PEOPLE

THE WETHERBEES

ACKNOWLEDGEMENTS

I WANT TO thank the following for their support of my work and this book:

Mary Ann Mroczka, senior producer, *New Hampshire Chronicle*, WMUR-TV

Jeff Bartlett, general manager, WMUR-TV

Hearst Argyle, for allowing me to do this book

Rick Broussard, editor of *New Hampshire Magazine*, who got this project under way

Holly Scopa, Tracey Spolter, Chris Shepherd, Chris McDevitt, Paul Falco, Chris Orr, Brian Murphy and the rest of the *Chronicle* gang who make my on-air job easy

George Geers and Sara Minette of Plaidswede Publishing Co.

Laura for her love, support and suggestions

—Fritz Wetherbee

INTRODUCTION

HIS IS THE voice of New Hampshire.

Has been for years.

Fred Minot Wetherbee II weaves the tales of New Hampshire past and present—graves to lilacs, witches to generals, places you know, places you want to visit. He is known by one name—Fritz. So nicknamed because of the other Freds in the family—grandfather, father and a family friend. Thus, Fritz, another nickname for Fred. He is—and this is no surprise—11th generation Yankee, tracing his roots back to John Wetherbee, who landed in 1630 in Boston. His website, www.fritzwetherbee.com, will tell you all you need to know about the man—writer, cameraman, producer, voice.

The place where these stories are now born is in Acworth, where he is restoring a 200-year-old home. Books line the walls of his study, as do cameras, photos, mementos of theater, family and the other pursuits that intrigue him. Yes, that's an original portrait of Bette Davis in the corner , and, yes, Fritz did have a "run-on" with the actress. Read the story.

For years, the bespectacled bald man with "that voice" and that bow tie has held us spellbound for the little nuggets he tells of life in New Hampshire. And with those tales have come an Emmy or two . . . or three.

It is summer, and we have completed a morning of shooting photos for this book. At the cemetery in Milford, we are introduced to family—"I'm related to most everyone in here," he says. After a salute to the American flag, he looks across Route 101 and remembers who lived in that house over there and another boyhood chum who lived just up the street. Then we're up the street to the diner in this, his hometown, where an uncle used to bring him for breakfast on a Saturday morning.

The "we" are three—the storyteller, the publisher and Sara Minette, who served as an editor for this collection. We share memories of the past—the Spectras, politicos, and Durham days—remember, you saw him first on Channel 11, New Hampshire's public TV station.

It is Fritz who receives attention from the waitress, the cook—please sample this lemon meringue pie, she says—and then a customer who runs a shop across the street. The problem with dining with Fritz is a simple one, I say. I must be generous with the tip. Yes, you must, Fritz smiles, as his coffee cup is filled yet again.

Read these stories, and you will hear Fritz's voice. Don't take my word for it—read what Jud Hale says on the back cover. In fact, most of what you read here was once a segment for *New Hampshire Chronicle* on WMUR-TV in Manchester.

Are these stories real?

As real as the town history books from which he gleans his material.

As real as any good story garnished to delight the listener—and reader.

All true. Of course.

Some with a touch of myth. Absolutely.

And all told by New Hampshire's master storyteller . . . with a wink of the eye.

Enjoy Fritz.

—George Geers, publisher, Plaidswede

FRITZ WETHERBEE'S
NEW HAMPSHIRE

THE STORIES

Uncle Sam

WHAT DO YOU know about Uncle Sam . . . that is, the Uncle Sam that is the symbol of the United States?

Did you know he was a real person?

Well, he was, and he grew up in Mason. His name was Sam Wilson.

Uncle Sam was actually born in what is now Arlington, Mass., in 1766, but he moved to Mason with his mother, father, eight brothers and two sisters when he was 14 years old.

Sam Wilson lived in a house in Mason. He lived here until he was 23. He fell in love with a Mason girl, Betsy Mann, whose dad owned the general store.

Betsy, they say, also had another suitor who had asked for her hand, a little guy who lived on a farm just over the border near Fitchburg. His name was John Chapman, and he was only 16 at the time, so he didn't have much of a chance. It is said that it was Betsy's refusal that sent him out of New England. It was, they say, a broken heart that sent him on his way.

Betsy and Sam Wilson were married and, in 1789, Sam, with his brother, Eban, moved to Troy, N.Y. There they set up a brick-making business, which made them a lot of money, and the two became leading citizens in Troy.

People called them, affectionately, "Uncle Eban" and "Uncle Sam" Wilson.

In 1783, Uncle Eban and Uncle Sam established a meat-packing business and slaughterhouse in Troy. When the War of 1812 broke out, the "E. and S. Wilson Packing Company" was chosen to supply the U.S. Army with barrels of corned beef.

This was the first time the United States had fought a war as an independent country and the government required all barrels of beef to be stamped with initials, "U.S."

Literally thousands of barrels were shipped from the Troy packing plant.

The joke in Troy was that the U.S. stood for Uncle Sam Wilson.

Troops would say, "more meat from Uncle Sam," and, pretty soon, all things delivered to the army with those initials were referred to as "from Uncle Sam."

People wrote poems about Uncle Sam. The Hutchinson Family Singers from Milford presented a popular song which ended with the words: "Uncle Sam is rich enough to give us all a farm."

But it wasn't until Uncle Sam Wilson was 85 years old that the character we know of as Uncle Sam was created, that is, the visual character.

And here's how this came about. Seems there was a big parade in Amesbury, Mass., in 1851. A Scottish-born man with chin whiskers, one George Buchanan, appeared in that parade, wearing a tall hat with big buttons sewn all around the band and striped trousers . . . with a sign calling himself, "Uncle Sam."

So there you have it. There was an artist at the parade from *Leslie's Illustrated Weekly*. And he drew the character and the caption was "Uncle Sam."

The country loved it. The rest is history.

But in the beginning there was, as I say, a real Uncle Sam.

Oh, I almost forgot Betsy Mann's other suitor, John Chapman. John became an expert in horticulture, specifically fruit. He traveled the country preaching the gospel and planting trees. You probably know of him. He was called Johnny Appleseed.

Can you believe it? Johnny Appleseed and Uncle Sam both in love with the same woman? And it all happened in Mason, New Hampshire, to boot! ❧

Fascinating gravestones

AS YOU PROBABLY know, I am fascinated by graveyards and grave-stones—especially those that tell a story.

In Marlboro, in the Street graveyard, there is a pitiful story, told simply.

Here is the grave of Patty Ward, a 5½-year-old girl who died in 1795.

The stone reads:

> *By boiling cider she was slain*
> *Whilst less than six of age*
> *Then her exquisite racking pain*
> *Removed her from the stage*
> *But her immortal spirit went*
> *to the Almighty King*
> *Where all the Godly ones are sent*
> *The praise of God to sing . . .*

In the same yard is the grave of Martin Van Buren—not the eighth president of the United States but, rather, an adopted 8 year old who died in 1845.

The city of Keene, too, has some interesting cemeteries and stones.

On Washington Street is one of the oldest graveyards in town and, just inside the gates, is the stone to Seth Newcomb, who died in 1811. The Keene City History notes that Seth was the fourth of 10 children born to John and Sarah Newcomb . . . that a brother, George, had drowned in the Ashuelot River at the age of 13 when Seth was 10 . . . and that he graduated Harvard and practiced law in Keene. It does not say that he was a hard-drinking hellion who died young . . . but his tombstone does. It reads:

> *. . . his life, though short, was active, too much devoted,*
> *however, to the world and too little to his maker . . .*

The stone tells us, however, that he was converted during his fatal illness.

In the North Cemetery in Keene is this sad tombstone that says: In Memory of Stephen, son of Lt. Stephen Chase and Mrs. Betsy, his wife. He died June 8, 1797, in the 7th year of his age, whose death was occasioned by a fall of a tree. How short the span, short from the cradle to the grave.

And, right behind this stone is, perhaps, the Yankee-est of all Yankee tombstones in New England. It reads:

Zilpah Kilburn 1804

And then down below we have:

Made by Moses Wright of Rockingham.
Price, six dollars. ✒

Done the best she could

IN THE GRAND colonial cemetery in Jaffrey Center lie the bones of many noted people. The African slave Amos Fortune is buried here, as is the great female entrepreneur Hannah Davis, and the Pulitzer Prize-winning author Willa Cather.

But amid the town founders, patriots and the famous, lies a grave of such humility as to break the heart.

Here is the grave of Sarah Averill, whose life is summed up with modesty so great that it in itself is memorable. It reads:

She done the best she could.

In the Phillips Cemetery in Jaffrey's West Burying Ground, there sits a gravestone that is carved in the shape of a large, comfortable armchair.

This is the great stone chair, a memorial to the Ross family, whose hospitality was well known when they lived—and continues after death.

"Come and rest," they say. And ponder that great rest to come. ✑

Garfield's grandfather

MY GRANDMOTHER REMEMBERED James Abram Garfield's assassination. It was one of her earliest memories. She was 13 years old. She told me that the entire town of Milford was draped in black crepe.

Oh, you know who James Garfield was, don't you? No, he is not a cartoon cat. James Garfield was the 20th president of the United States. And James A. Garfield had a direct connection with New Hampshire.

His mother was born and came from Richmond . . . over near Keene. Garfield's maternal grandfather was one James Ballou and, in fact, the president was named for him.

In his early adulthood James Garfield came to Richmond to write a family genealogy and history. This story I am about to tell you is from that history.

Seems Garfield's grandfather was a very smart man. He was a mathematician, and he studied astrology. James Ballou could predict when any planets would be in alignment.

People came from all over to have their horoscopes read and James Ballou made a fine living doing it. Whether or not he really believed in astrology is not known, but his puckish sense of humor is known.

A case in point:

It seems that one day a bunch of rich college boys arrived at the Ballou home in a very fancy carriage. They moved into the Ballou home and commandeered rooms and food. All of them let the family know how much better they were than the hicks in Richmond. They were, in short, insufferable. And they did a very stupid thing: they angered James Ballou.

The next day, after he had read all their horoscopes, the boys were ordering people to load up their carriage for their trip back to Boston when one of them remembered that James Ballou had a reputation for being able to conjure up the devil . . . Satan himself, and they ordered him to do it. They wanted to see Beelzebub personally.

Well, James Ballou warned them that this was nothing to be taken lightly.

The sight of the devil had been known to drive men mad and that they had better be ready for the test. This just made them more insistent.

And so, James Ballou waited 'til dark. He seated the boys in a dark room. He then began his mystical incantations.

Soon, far away, there was a "thump . . . thump!"

Ballou continued to chant. The thumping got louder and louder. It was the devil approaching. The boys started to get jittery.

James Ballou then told them that if the sight of the devil was too frightful the boys were to shout at the top of their lungs, "LAY HIM! LAY HIM!"

The thumping became tremendous . . . just outside the door. Then it was quiet.

No one took a breath.

And then the door burst open and the boys beheld a hideous sight.

"LAY HIM! LAY HIM!" they shouted.

The Prince of Darkness stood at the door. It was the most horrible thing they had ever seen. "LAY HIM!" they shouted, and James Ballou waved his hand and the apparition disappeared.

Inside the room, everyone was gasping from the horror. Outside the room, James' brother, Russell, was hiding his outlandish costume in its accustomed place.

And the next day, James said, you never saw a finer or better behaved bunch of boys that got aboard their carriage bound for Boston. ◆

The Devil and John Stark

This statue of General Stark is in front of the Statehouse in Concord.

BETWEEN NEW BOSTON and Weare, there is an area of wetlands called "The Great Cedar Swamp."

It was in this area where the Revolutionary War hero John Stark once went hunting with a friend and met the devil.

The story is in the Manchester City History. Unfortunately, it does not tell us the friend's name, but it does say he came from Massachusetts.

The two men were deer hunting and had stayed hailing distance from each other so as not to be shot by mistake. A short way into the swamp, General Stark's friend said, in a subdued voice, "Stark, Stark, come here."

Supposing his friend had seen a moose or a deer, the General replied, "What do you see?"

His friend said, in an even lower voice, "The Devil." And at that moment he fired his musket.

General Stark rushed forward and there at the feet of his friend lay a giant wildcat writhing in the agonies of death.

The friend had looked up to see the cat in the lower branches of a tree just ahead of him. He had called the general for assistance but, before he could come, the cat leapt. The man pulled the trigger of his musket and shot the beast in mid-air right between the eyes. The leap was measured at over 30 feet.

General Stark was impressed with his friend's shooting ability. Looking the man in the eye, General Stark said, "Well, I guess you'll do."

No mean compliment, they tell me. ·•

The Dunbar House

ASA DUNBAR HAD health problems all his life. He was born in Bridgewater, Mass., in 1745. His family had money. Asa graduated from Harvard where he studied for the ministry.

His first parish was in Salem, Mass. The congregation there liked him . . . but he was sick a lot and had to resign.

He left Massachusetts and came north to Amherst, where he read law. Then, as a lawyer, he settled in Keene.

Asa Dunbar was as good a lawyer as he had been a preacher. Soon he had a thriving practice. His best friend was the attorney Daniel Jones of Hinsdale.

Daniel had a sister, Mary. And Mary and Asa fell in love. The couple married and had six children in as many years, the youngest of whom they named Cynthia.

But, alas, Asa Dunbar was not to see his family grown. He took sick and died. It was just one month after Cynthia was born.

Mary Dunbar was now on her own. To provide for her family, she opened a rooming house and tavern. For years it was called the Dunbar House.

Mary outlived her husband by 50 years. To the end, she lived in the tavern.

Her youngest daughter, Cynthia, grew into a vivacious, large-boned woman who they say had opinions.

Cynthia married a man from Concord, Mass. The couple had four children whom they named, respectively, Helen, John (after his father. Cynthia's husband was John), David, and the youngest, Sophia.

The family was respected in Concord, Mass., but they were very poor. The father, John, had a modest wooden pencil manufacturing business.

The younger son, David, was a loner and an excellent scholar. He attended Harvard where he mastered Greek, Latin, Italian, French, German and Spanish.

He also loved the out-of-doors. He walked everywhere, including trips to the Monadnock region where he would climb Mt. Monadnock and then walk over to Keene to visit his grandmother.

Now I have, in some way, been misleading you. It is true that Mary Dunbar's grandson had been christened, "David," but his family, and most people, called him by his middle name and he published books under that name, "Henry."

We are talking, of course, of Henry David Thoreau, the great author of *Civil Disobedience* and *Walden Pond* and close friend with the Alcotts and Ralph Waldo Emerson.

And a note here.

Henry's mother, Cynthia, and Ralph Waldo Emerson did not like one another. Cynthia thought him arrogant and a bad influence on Henry. And Emerson detested Cynthia. There is a story that Emerson once came to call on Henry in Concord and Cynthia answered the door.

Emerson immediately turned his back on the woman and would not speak to her. Cynthia, for her part, turned her back on Emerson and the two stood, arms crossed and looking in opposite directions until Henry arrived to lead his friend Emerson away.

The old tavern, The Dunbar House, still exists on Main Street in Keene. Today it is a "Margaritas." Back in the '80s, the owners called it "Henry David's" and claimed it to be the oldest continuously operated restaurant in America. ❧

The last wolf on Monadnock

IN 1819, IN the entire area between Mt. Watatic in Massachusetts and Mt. Monadnock in New Hampshire, there was only one wolf left of the thousands that had roamed the area only 50 years before.

No one knew back then about ecology or species' extinction. Back then, trees and wolves were enemies, and the sooner they were eliminated, the better.

Back then, most of the trees had been cut off Mt. Monadnock. Pastureland covered two-thirds of the mountain. Pastures, of course, meant sheep and cows, and they were easy pickings for the wolf packs that roamed the area.

But in the winter of 1819–1820, a single wolf roamed the Monadnock region, and one day, a dozen hunters with their hounds gathered in Fitzwilliam. Their purpose was to find and kill the last remaining wolf.

They trailed the wolf into Jaffrey, then back again into Fitzwilliam and down into Winchendon and then north into Rindge. On the third day, they ended their hunt at the farm of Phineas Whitney in Fitzwilliam and, while they slept in the house, the wolf got into the Whitney barn and killed three sheep . . . apparently just for sport, as very little was eaten of the carcasses. The men in the house were awakened by the hubbub and managed to fire on the wolf as it fled. But the animal escaped unharmed. For nine days, the bloodhounds tracked the wolf.

On the second Sunday of the hunt, the dogs were driving the wolf from Fitzwilliam toward Monadnock. Word was out that they finally had the wolf. Every man in town turned out and lined the road between Fitzwilliam and Jaffrey.

In the shadow of Monadnock, the animal was driven into Scott Meadow where Shubel Plimpton got off a shot and hit it. Lewis Robbins of Fitzwilliam got off the second shot, but the animal refused to go down. It took three bullets to finally kill the wolf.

The wolf was heisted on poles and carried back to Fitzwilliam, where it was paraded around the common to the cheers of those who turned out. There had been no church that day.

And that's the story of the last wolf on Monadnock. ❧

Captain Salter and the ferry

OUT WHERE THE New Castle Bridge connects the city of Portsmouth with Shapely Islands, there used to sit a handsome house belonging to Captain John Salter.

Back before the American Revolution, Captain Salter was renowned for his sailing skill, his bravery and his resourcefulness.

At one time, the captain sailed out of Portsmouth Harbor bound for London with a trunk full of Spanish doubloons. Off the coast of Maine, his ship ran into a storm which drove it onto the rocks off the Kennebec River.

Due to the skill of the captain, the ship managed to make land. There the captain saw the ship repaired. Months later, he completed the voyage. It wasn't until the ship returned over a year later that anyone here knew of its fate.

Captain Salter was held in great respect in the community. There is a story about his youth that is told by Charles Brewster in his 1859 publication of his *Rambles*. The story is:

When Captain Salter was a young boy, a stranger came to his home at Frame Point and asked the boy to row him across the bay to New Castle. This, of course, was before there was a bridge.

The stranger was imperious and a wind bag, and young John Salter was on his guard at once.

Nothing was said about payment for being rowed across the point.

Nevertheless the two started off; young John rowing and the fancy-dressed man regaling him with how important a passenger he had.

Instead of going straight to New Castle, the young ferryman rowed his boat to the beach at Goat Island. His passenger thought he was at New Castle. And so he leapt ashore.

He then bowed to the lad and walked up the beach. Then he turned and said, "I shall pay you when we meet in town some day."

Young Salter began rowing away. Just then, the stranger looked around and discovered that he was the only person on a very small island.

"Young man, young man," he yelled, "come back!"

Continuing to row, the future Captain Salter waved back and said, "Oh, perhaps we shall meet in town some day."

And he rowed away whistling. ❧

A comical death

IN THE NORTH central part of the town of Temple lies a 400-acre tract of land known as the Borland Farm. It is named for an American Tory who died during the Battle of Bunker Hill.

You say there were no American Tories at the Battle of Bunker Hill, only American Patriots and British troops? True. But I did not say Mr. Borland died fighting in the battle, only that he died during it. The story is in the *Temple Town History*.

The history, by the way, makes no mention of Mr. Borland's first name, so we will call him simply, "Mr. Borland."

His family, as I say, owned land in what is now Temple but he, Mr. Borland, lived mostly in Boston and he hated the Patriots. He was a Tory through and through.

During the Battle of Bunker Hill (which actually was, as you know, fought on Breed's Hill) . . . during the battle, he mounted to the roof of a house "to see the damn rebels fall!"

The rebels did fall that day (or rather ran out of ammunition and had to quit) but so did Mr. Borland. Not quit, but fall.

You see, while he was cheering the British on, the railing on the rooftop gave way and Mr. Borland fell to his death. His last words were not recorded, probably only a scream . . . one of many that day. ✜

Here lies the amputated leg

IT'S LIKE A great first sentence that pulls you headlong into a story. But it is not the first sentence in a story. It is, instead, a gravestone. It reads:

Captain Samuel Jones' leg, which was amputated July 7, 1804.

In TV, you'd call this inscription 'a tease.' In songwriting, you'd call it 'the hook.' It's that thing that you can't ignore.

The frustrating part is that there is only a first sentence. Paul Harvey would be disappointed because there is no "rest of the story."

Oh, yes, there is black comedy here. You wonder, did they have a funeral for the appendage? Was there a coffin? Was there a minister? What text did he quote? Who attended? And just who was this Samuel Jones? What'd he look like? How'd he lose his leg? And, most importantly, where is the rest of him?

When you stand on this grave, it is difficult not to picture a shinbone and foot moldering away beneath this stone.

So, here we have the greatest first line since "Call me Ishmael" and very little else.

What I could find is this:

The 'Capt.' part of Capt. Sam was because he was an officer in the town militia. Seems Captain Sam was moving a house and it got away from him and crushed his leg. The house can still be seen; it's across from the General Store.

No doubt a lot of rum was involved in the amputation. And, by the way, before antibiotics and such, amputations were regularly done when there was a compound fracture . . . else the patient would probably die of blood poisoning.

Anyhow, right after the amputation, the good captain moved out of town, worked at the Customs House in Boston for a number of years and then went to the Customs House in New York City. No one knows where he's buried.

The graveyard with the leg, however, can be found. It's on the left about a 100 yards down the street behind the town gazebo. You can't miss it. ☙

Insanity defense

WE THINK OF the insanity defense as something quite recent, but did you know that the insanity defense was first argued in New Hampshire way back in 1834?

The defendant was an 18-year-old boy who smashed in the skull of a woman on a farm in North Pembroke. The boy was one Abraham Prescott. Today he would probably be regarded as mildly retarded. Back then he was said to be slow.

He was taken into a family in North Pembroke to be a hired boy . . . an apprentice. The family consisted of a husband and wife, Chauncey and Sally Cochran, their two small children, and Chauncey's aged mother.

Abraham lived in the house with the family. He fed the livestock, milked the cows, ran the ox team. . . . He was, by all accounts, a likable boy.

Abraham Prescott lived with the Cochrans three years. And then one January night he did something awful. He came into Sally and Chauncey's bedroom and with an ax hacked away at the couple as they slept. He then called for the grandmother and said that he didn't know what had happened. He had, he said, been sleepwalking.

The amazing thing was that the family bought it. The grandmother sent for the medical examiner, Dr. Sargent, who questioned the boy and backed him up; he had been sleepwalking. Chauncey and Sally had some pretty serious cuts to the sides of their heads, but they recovered.

Now what the Cochrans did next seems puzzling. They, in fact, did nothing. Abraham Prescott continued to live with the family. They forgave him.

Five and a half months later—June 23, 1833—Abraham told Sally that he had found some wild strawberries in a meadow down by what was then called Great Brook.

At eight o'clock that morning she went with him to the meadow. Minutes later he appeared back at the house to say that Sally was dead.

The coroner and police came again. They found Sally Cochran lying on her back in the meadow, her head bashed in. A bloody fence stake was on the ground beside her.

Major Stimson of the Concord police asked Abraham what had happened, and he said he had been sleepwalking again.

"Sleepwalking, again?" Stimson said, "That just won't do!"

Abraham Prescott then confessed. He had beaten Sally to death. To this day we do not know why he killed her. At the time it was thought that he had made improper advances and she had rebuffed him and told him he was a bad boy and would no longer be able to stay with them.

Abraham Prescott was charged with first-degree murder and jailed in Concord. The trial began in September of 1834. It was held in the North Church in Concord.

Two attorneys, Ichabod Bartlett of Portsmouth and Charles Peasley of Concord, represented Abraham Prescott. They pled their client "Not guilty by reason of insanity."

New Hampshire then, as now, was the only state in the union that had no definition for "insanity." "Insanity" was, in other words, whatever a jury decided it might be.

Why insanity? Well, for one reason, Abraham Prescott's grandfather (also called Abraham) was known to be mad. A family friend, Hezekiah Blake, testified to that.

Abraham's mother, Mary Prescott, testified that her son had been born when she was 56 and that he had a big head, so big that when he was three years old, he wore the same-size hat as his father. From the time he was born, she said, the child was covered with a rash and acted oddly. She and her husband took the boy to the ocean to bathe him in the salt water, but nothing seemed to help.

The jury didn't buy it. They found Abraham Prescott guilty.

But the jury had been sloppy. During the deliberations, they had discussed the trial at a local barber shop. Abraham Prescott's lawyers filed for a mistrial and got one. But the verdict did not change.

Abraham Prescott was taken to the jail in Hopkinton to await his hanging.

In the meantime, there was a lot of political pressure to change his sentence and, in fact, the governor did stay the first date in December of 1835.

The result was a lynch mob marching on the jail. The jailer's wife pleaded with the mob not to kill the prisoner. Her daughter, she said, had just given birth and was very sick. The emotion might kill her. The mob went away to the Perkins Hotel. There they hanged Prescott in effigy. Three days later, on the day after Christmas, the jailer's daughter did die.

A year went by. On the sixth of January, 1836, ten thousand people crowded the roads into Hopkinton. A gallows had been constructed at the base of a natural amphitheater near the center of town.

A fife and drum preceded a wagon carrying the coffin the condemned man would leave in. Behind the coffin, in another wagon, rode Abraham Prescott.

He was lead to the platform. His hands and legs were bound with leather straps, a bag was placed over his head and the struts kicked out under the trap.

And Abraham Prescott was ushered into eternity.

The body was allowed to hang a half-hour and then was taken away. No one nowadays seems to know where. Some say it is an unmarked grave in Pembroke. Others say friends took the body to Rumney, Vermont. But the common belief is that, because Abraham Prescott's only request at his execution was that his body not be cut up, it was taken to Hanover and used as a cadaver at the Dartmouth Medical School.

Today you cannot find Abraham Prescott, but you can find Sally Cochran.

Sacred to her memory, it says on the tombstone, she was inhumanly murdered. ❧

Man kills bear with bare hands

WE ALL ARE familiar with stories of wolves attacking children and other human beings—Little Red Riding Hood and all that; throwing the baby from the troika in order to outrun the wolf pack. Scary stories.

But the fact is, in New England, at least, no human was ever killed by wolves. Wildcats could be dangerous if cornered, but there too, there is no history of one ever killing a human being in New England. These creatures killed livestock—sheep, pigs, chickens, but not people.

Bears, however, were a different story. A grizzly mother with cubs will charge any animal she deems a threat. To this day, we hear stories about campers eaten in their sleeping bags by bears; kind of the ursine version of a hot dog in a roll.

New Hampshire town histories are full of stories about people being mauled by bears.

One of my favorites is in the *Rindge Town History*.

It's a story of a man who was mauled by a bear, but finally managed to kill it. And here's the best part: he killed it with his own hands without a weapon. In fact, he killed it with only one hand! The event happened about 1799.

Deacon Lovejoy set a bear trap in the woods near his home in Rindge. The trap was attached to a large log with a draft chain. Sure enough, he caught a bear in the trap. Now in those days gunpowder was expensive and the good deacon, being a Yankee, decided to save money and dispatch the bear, not by shooting it, but with an ax.

Big mistake.

Also, when Deacon Lovejoy went back to the trap, his son, a 7 year old, accompanied him. The boy watched as his father approached the bear.

His dad raised the weapon and slammed it down.

The bear dodged the blow. Not only that, but the bear slammed the ax out of his hand. It then grasped the deacon by the arm and drew him down.

The boy came to his father's aid and began to pull at the bear but the bear then pulled the boy to him, also.

Oh, now the bear had both the boy and his father and was about to rip them apart. It opened its great mouth and, at that moment, Deacon Lovejoy did a desperate thing: he presented his fist to the bear's mouth. The bear opened up and the good deacon thrust his fist into the mouth and down the throat. The bear was choking. It pushed at the man. It tried to run. It thrashed. And then it choked to death.

Deacon Lovejoy's arm was chewed and torn. It would never be useful again. But it would heal and it did. And the deacon lived a long and happy life. ☙

Bear leaves man bare

AS THEY SAY, sometimes you get the bear ... and sometimes the bear gets you.

Well, the old *Hancock Town History* has a story of a man who almost got the bear and the bear almost got him.

The man's name was Josiah Stone Senior and he was living on the Jonathan Bennett farm in Hancock when all this happened. The time was 1790.

The history tells us that Mr. Stone had some lambs and pigs missing. At the time he didn't know what kind of a predator he was dealing with, but he suspected a bear. But it could have been foxes.

Either way, Josiah Stone filled his muzzle loader with a moderate amount of shot and with his dog set out to deal with his livestock killer. In his sheep pasture, he confronted a bear, took aim and pulled the trigger. The weapon fired and the shot hit its mark, but the bear didn't go down. Instead the bear was enraged and charged. Josiah Stone ran, the bear after him, and the dog after the bear.

As he attempted to get over a large log, the bear got hold of him and was about to pull him down when the dog got hold of the bear's leg. The bear turned and, in doing so, tore most of Josiah Stone's clothing off. Naked, he ran from the woods like blazes. The dog, too, got away.

Needless to say the dog was kept by the family and treated well until it died finally of old age. ·❧

Man's best friend

IN MONT VERNON, about half way into the town cemetery there is
a grave that reads:

William C. Bruce
Born Feb 1, 1819
Accidentally Shot While Hunting
Oct 27, 1883

An intriguing monument, as it has a violent death and tells a story—albeit an incomplete one. But even more intriguing is what is
behind this stone. For here there is a life-sized statue of a hound dog
lying over his master's grave. There is no name on the statue nor a
date nor a reason why it is here.

Here's the story:

Bill Bruce, it seems, was out bird hunting when he tripped and
accidentally shot himself. His dog remained at his side as he died
and remained there for some hours until his barking lead searchers
to where his master lay.

Bill's wife, Augusta, was so moved by the fidelity of the old hound
that at the dog's death she traveled to Peterborough and had monu-
ment-maker Hubert Bremman carve the effigy of her husband's best
friend to lie eternally here at his side.

The dog is not buried here. That's against the law, and maybe it's
a shame.

And we don't know the dog's name. But we do know what he or
she looked like. ✒

Lincoln's favorite band

OF ALL THE musical groups to play during the Civil War, none had greater renown than Abraham Lincoln's favorite, The Port Royal Band.

This 24-member marching band was the most-documented musical group in the Union Army.

It was known to have the best musicians and the best marchers and, to the great glory of the citizens of the Granite State, the band was also known under its original designation, "The Third New Hampshire Regimental Band."

All the members of Lincoln's favorite band came from Concord and the towns close by. ♣

The Beaneaters

DID YOU EVER hear of the Boston Beaneaters?

Well, to clear things up, the Beaneaters were first called the Boston Red Stockings. They were one of the first National League teams, founded in 1876, and, in fact, played the first National League game. In that game, they beat the Philadelphia Athletics, 6–5, in Philly on April 22 of that year.

In 1883, however, they changed their name to the Boston Braves. This was to avoid confusion between the Boston Red Stockings and the Cincinnati Reds of the American Association.

A lot of famous people wore the Braves uniform—Roger Hornsby and Jim Thorpe, even Babe Ruth finished his career as a Brave.

In 1936 the team changed its name again . . . to the Boston Bees. In 1941, they went back to the name, Braves.

So, there you have it. You probably can tell me the rest of the story: In 1953, they moved out of Boston to . . . no, not Atlanta . . . but to Milwaukee.

It was with the Milwaukee team that Hank Aaron won his batting title. It was 1965 when the team moved to Atlanta.

But the original old Beaneaters were one heck of a team. They, in fact, won five pennants, and the credit for their success was given to their manager, a guy named Frank Selee. And Frank Selee came . . . you can say it with me . . . from New Hampshire. Right. Born and grew up in Amherst.

If all Frank Selee had done was manage the old Boston Beaneaters, he still would have a major place in Baseball History. But Frank Selee did more. In 1890, he went to the Chicago Cubs. When he took over, the team had the worst record in the league. But over the next 16 years, under Frank Selee management, the team fashioned a .598 winning percentage, the fourth highest of all time.

But Frank Selee is remembered also in poetry, a poem about the most-noted double play combination in the history of the game. A combination he put together.

The poem was written in 1910 by newspaper columnist; Franklin

Pierce Adams (another New Hampshire connection) and it is entitled: BASEBALL'S SAD LEXICON.

The trio of Cubs who made such great double plays were infielders Joe Tinker, Johnny Evers and Frank Chance. Over the years, they beat the poet's beloved New York Giants over and over again.

The poem he wrote goes like this:

> *These are the saddest of possible words*
> *Tinker to Evers to Chance*
> *Trio of bear cubs, and fleeter than birds*
> *Tinker to Evers to Chance*
> *Ruthlessly pricking our gonfalon bubble*
> *Making a Giant hit into a double*
> *Words that are heavy with nothing but trouble*
> *Tinker to Evers to Chance.*

Frank Selee is one of two New Hampshire men who are in the Baseball Hall of Fame, the other being, of course, Carlton Fisk. So let's remember Frank Selee . . . for great baseball . . . and some memorable poetry. ✒

Fourth of July in Peterborough

FOR YEARS THE kids in Hancock used to ring in the Fourth of July by ringing the church bell at the meeting house.

It was common to do this in all the towns in America.

Hancock put a stop to the practice a couple dozen years ago because the kids got too rowdy. It had gotten out of hand and the pulling privilege was, well, it was pulled.

The same thing happened over in Peterborough way back in 1870. And, in fact, the town constable was posted to see that no young men would get in to pull the bell. But somehow, the bell was rung that night, and here's how it was done:

The town constable was a man named Theophilus Parsons Ames. 'Parse' was, by all accounts, a good guy with a good sense of humor, but he would brook no shenanigans from the youngsters in town.

So the night before the Fourth of July, he sat himself down on the steps of the Unitarian church. Anybody with any idea of ringing the bell would have to get by him. Now tradition was that the bell would be tolled on the stroke of midnight so Parse's job would, he thought, be easy.

Well, about half past ten a bunch of young fellows came up to Parse on the steps and stood around telling jokes and stories. Parse noted the time and said they probably should be home in bed.

Oh, no, they said, they weren't tired at all!

Suddenly there was a great ruckus up on Grove Street, a lot of yelling and screaming bloody murder and Parse and the young men all went up to investigate. The yelling seemed to be coming from down by the river, but when they got there, there was no one and Parse knew he'd been had—they'd gotten him away from the church. He expected the bell to ring on his way back to his post.

But it didn't. So he took up his vigil again. Then midnight came and the town bell chimed out 12 strokes, and then 13 . . . and 14 . . . and 15. In fact, the town clock continued to ring non-stop for an hour.

"What in the blue blazes is the matter with that clock?" said Parse.

Well, one of the boys mentioned that his dad said one of the ratchets on the clock was badly worn and was liable to break at any time and, if it did, it would probably strike until it ran down.

What happened, of course, was that a couple boys climbed up into the clock tower and tied some clothesline to the clapper of the bell and threw the rope down to the street. At the same time, some boys climbed into the tower of the Baptist church across the way and also threw down some clothesline. The two ropes were tied together and the boys sat in the Baptist church tower and waited for midnight.

The only reason the ringing stopped was that the rope finally sawed itself through on the Unitarian side where the rope went around a shutter.

The janitor found a few hundred feet of clothesline in the Baptist belfry a few days later. And a great many housewives went out that Monday to hang out their wash and found nothing to hang it on. ❧

The largest American flag

AMERICA ENTERED WORLD War I in April of 1917, but we had been preparing for the entry into the war for some months.

In fact, a full year before, in May of 1916, there had been a March of Preparedness in New York City. It was the largest civic parade in United States history up to that time.

For this event, the Amoskeag Mills in Manchester created the largest American flag ever made before or since.

It was 100 feet long and 52 feet wide and weighed a full 500 pounds and was carried by the marchers, not from a pole, but held flat by the edges and could only be seen to great advantage from the tall buildings along Broadway. ❧

Public floggings

AH, THE GOOD old days: no TV, no CDs . . .

But there were compensations. For instance, public floggings. Well into the 19th century, whipping was common punishment for minor offenses: petty thievery, assault.

People turned out for floggings as entertainment.

It wasn't until the end of the Civil War that states recognized that cruelty begets only more cruelty, and that whippings were barbarous, and did away with them.

The old *Wilton Town History* has a story of a public flogging.

To quote from the history:

"An oak on the Wilton common was in the early times the whipping-post. A culprit, condemned to undergo the punishment for stealing clothes hung out to dry, made his shrieks heard across the valley a mile away. An old lady relates that at a later period a whipping-post, eight or ten feet high, stood at the southeast corner of the common. Here justice was administered on violators of the law and disturbers of the peace of the community."

The same post, the town history tells us, was also used as a bulletin board for public notices. ❧

Fighting teacher

IF YOU WATCH television, no doubt you know that kids today are tougher, more dangerous, and more impolite than kids used to be.

"When I was in school we had to behave. It's not like nowadays." That's what my dad used to say. I've said the same thing to my son and he has kids now.

I guess you get the drift. Memory is selective. A case in point: back in the year 1900, the kids in the Hancock Central School had gotten so unruly that three teachers in a row resigned.

It was so drastic a situation that the district supervisor went looking for a teacher who could not only teach, but also fight. He found a man named Harry E. Gardner. Gardner had not yet graduated from normal school (back then teachers' colleges were called 'normal schools'). Harry Gardner was attending school and, at the same time, had a full-time job making shoes in a Bridgewater, Mass., factory. The headmaster of the normal school recommended him because he was athletic and tough and fast. He was also, the headmaster said, a great student.

So, at the start of the winter semester, Harry Gardner stood in front of the Hancock school watching a bunch of unruly teens sauntering up to the door. They formed a circle around the new man.

"So, you're the new teacher?" said one.

"I am," said Harry.

"Well, I bet I can rub your face on the floor," said the tough kid.

"You are welcome to try," said Harry.

The young bully attempted to grab the new teacher, but Mr. Gardner was too fast for him. He whirled him around and caught him by the scuff of the neck and the seat of the pants and proceeded to toss him into a snow bank.

And Mr. Harry E. Gardner, teacher of the central school in Hancock, had no trouble at all from any student for the entire time he taught there. ❧

The pine tree riot

THE FIRST ACT of rebellion of the American Revolution was the Boston Tea Party. The first battle was the "shot heard round the world" at Lexington and Concord. Except in New Hampshire history. In New Hampshire, we know that the first battle was at Fort William and Mary in New Castle.

And the first act of rebellion occurred in Weare. Maybe you haven't heard this story:

In 1722, King George the First made it a penal offense to cut any tree over 12 inches as measured three feet from the ground. Fines ranged from five to 50 pounds and the forfeit of the cut trees. It was pay up or go to prison. No one paid much attention to the law.

In 1764, Governor Benning Wentworth, in his grant for the incorporation of Weare, put a tree clause in the town charter. But as long as there were enough trees when they were called for, the law was generally ignored. Benning Wentworth resigned in 1766 and his nephew John Wentworth replaced him.

John saw at once that there could be a lot of money in collecting the fines and enforcing licenses. He set about doing just that.

A king's deputy was sent around to place arrows on all trees reserved for the king. Anyone wanting to cut other trees now had to have a license. If you already cut any trees, it was going to cost you a lot of money. Too much money. The king's deputies even fined settlers for the white pine logs in the walls of their cabins.

To say these guys were hated is to understate the point. Even the town meeting houses were not exempt. The deputies would show up at millyards and walk around putting the king's arrow on trees. These trees were seized. If the mill owner could not pay, the logs were sold at auction. The money, of course, went to John Wentworth and His Majesty's treasury.

John Shelburne was one of the governor's deputies. He rode into the Piscataquog Valley in the winter of 1771–72. He found illegal logs at Richard's Mill, Pattee's Mill and at Dow's Mill. He found 270 illegal logs at Clement's Mill in the Oil Mill Village of Weare.

The vice-admiralty court in Boston summoned the mill owners to appear. A local lawyer, Samuel Blodget, Esq., of Goffstown, was sent to Portsmouth by the mill owners to defend their interests.

Blodget made a deal with the governor. He said he could never get the entire amount from his clients, but he could get a lot of money if he were given freedom to negotiate.

The governor liked the proposal and made Blodget a deputy surveyor of the King's Woods. The job came with a handsome commission. In other words, he bought him out.

On February 24, Blodget sent the mill owners a letter saying that they had caused him a disagreeable journey to Portsmouth and that they had better pay up. He said, however, that if they would call on him he would make the fines easier on them. In other words, he'd make a deal.

Three men from Bedford and 14 from Goffstown came at once, settled, and got their logs back; the men of Weare were obstinate. Warrants for their arrest were put in the hands of sheriff Benjamin Whiting, Esq., of Hollis. He was a hated man.

On April 13, Sheriff Whiting and a deputy, John Quigley of Francestown, came to Weare to arrest mill owner Ebenezer Mudgett, who lived in Oil Mill Village.

They found him late in the day and he agreed to meet with them the next day. The two sheriffs then repaired to Aaron Quimby's inn to spend the night.

That evening men from all over Weare gathered at the Mudgett home. At dawn, Mudgett slammed open the bedroom door of the sheriff and announced that the bail was ready to be paid. Sheriff Whiting rose and as he started to dress, chided Mudgett for coming so early. Just then, the door burst open again and more than 20 men rushed in. Their faces were blackened with charcoal and each held a switch in his hand.

Sheriff Whiting grabbed his pistol but the men were too fast for him. They disarmed him and then spread his arms and legs and held him face down just above the floor. They then beat him on the bare back with the switches. Later the sheriff was quoted as saying, "They almost killed me."

Deputy John Quigley, hearing the ruckus, locked his door. The men then went to the attic and pulled up the boards above the poor deputy. They poked down at him with long poles and finally got hold of him and beat him with switches just as they had his boss.

The mob then got the sheriff and deputy's horses, cropped their ears and cut off their manes and tails. This made the horses worthless. The two men were then forced to mount their horses and, as they rode down the road, the mob jeered and shouted at them.

The matter was not forgotten. One of the rioters was finally caught and, on September 8th, others were indicted. They were charged with making an assault on the body of Benjamin Whiting, Esq., so that he did "despair of his life." The men were arraigned before a panel of jurists. Most pleaded that they "would not contend with Our Lord the King but would submit themselves to his grace."

They were fined 20 shillings each and the cost of the prosecution.

It was a ridiculously light sentence and expressed the popular sentiment against the king's taxes and the particularly odious Pine Tree Law.

It was a time when England had imposed the Stamp Act and the Sugar Act and the tax on tea. But before these acts, there was the Pine Tree Riot in Weare.

Some say that this, and not the Boston Tea Party, was the first great act of defiance that led to the Revolutionary War.

The only reason the tea party is better known is because they had better historians. ☙

Amherst hanging

GEORGE GEERS PHOTOGRAPH

Fritz on the Amherst common

THE ONLY PUBLIC execution ever to occur in Hillsborough County happened on the Amherst common back in 1822.

The key word here is "public." After the first quarter of the century, executions took place behind the walls of the prisons and were not open to the general public.

But on January third of 1822, the one and only public execution in this county happened here, and it was standing room only.

The old Milford History tells us that the man executed was one Daniel D. Farmer of Goffstown. He killed a woman in his town named Mrs. Ayres, assaulted her daughter, left her for dead, and set fire to their house.

The daughter survived and testified against Mr. Farmer.

The day was cold but, nonetheless, over ten thousand people gathered here for the hanging. The county history says that virtually the entire adult population of the town turned out to witness the event. ❧

Griffin's Falls

ON DECEMBER 16, 1784, a terrible thing happened in Bedford.

That night, William McLaughlin had a big party to celebrate his recent marriage and the construction of his new home. People from all over Bedford and Derryfield were invited, and there was food and rum and a fiddler and dancing into the night.

Derryfield, in case you are new to New Hampshire, was what Manchester was originally called. Among the dozen-or-so people from Derryfield were Theophilus Griffin, his brother, John, John's wife and their friend, Abner Thompson.

To get to the celebration, these four had crossed the Merrimack River in a small boat. It being December, the night was cold and the three men and one woman were bundled up and carried blankets. It was late when they started back across the river and the men were, no doubt, none too sober. And, in fact, when the boat hit the current in the middle of the stream, it capsized.

Theophilus Griffin and his brother's wife clung to the upturned boat while John Griffin and his friend Abner Thompson made for shore. Both were strong swimmers. But the icy water soon overcame them and cramped their muscles, and both drowned.

Theophilus was also a strong swimmer but he clung to the craft and kicked toward shore. His brother's wife (and by the way, the town history does not record her name) could not swim and was soon unable to hold on to the boat. In her panic, she grabbed hold of her brother-in-law. This caused him to lose his grip and both went under. Theophilus kicked to the surface and again the woman grabbed him. This time he pushed her away and swam for the shore.

He made it and lay exhausted in the snow on the bank. Wet and frozen, he made his way back to the party where he told what had happened.

At daybreak, half the towns of Derryfield and Bedford were at the scene. Here they discovered the bodies of John Griffin and Abner Thompson.

The body of John's wife, however, was never recovered.

But the place in the river where the tragedy occurred is called to this day, "Griffin's Falls." ❧

Fence Viewers

FOR 250 YEARS now, the town of Peterborough has, at town meeting time, elected someone to the post of Fence Viewer.

Every four years or so someone proposes that the post of Fence Viewer be removed from the ballot as it costs money to print the ballots and the article in the town report and to count the votes for the position. As no one seems to know what Fence Viewers do, it is absurd to continue the post.

And each time this is suggested, it is voted down soundly. Remove the post of Fence Viewer? Never!

Each year there are half a dozen men or women who eagerly seek the position. With it, in Peterborough, by the way, goes a badge and a citation noting that the person is the Fence Viewer and should be treated accordingly.

Silliness aside, there did used to be a position of Fence Viewer in every town in New England. There were also the positions of Hog Reeves, Pound Keeper and Field Driver and Tithing Man, which people were elected to each year.

A Tithing Man saw to it that people went to church and observed proper order during services. If he found you had not been in church because you were playing cards, he could bring you to court and you would be punished. This was, of course, back before there was a separation between church and state.

The Pound Keeper was the official who was responsible for those rock-wall enclosures you see all over New England in the small towns. These enclosures were for locking up stray animals. Back then, if a cow or sheep or hog got off your farm and wandered onto the public common or on to someone else's land, then that animal was eating the grass that belonged to someone else and people didn't take kindly to it. The Pound Keeper would alert the Field Driver to go and round up the stray animal and put it in the pound. The pound had a stout door with a heavy lock and the Pound Keeper had the key. If you wanted your animal back, you had to pay the Pound Keeper a fine.

The Fence Viewer's job was to see that all the roads in the town had stone walls or fences on either side in order to keep animals on the road, if they were driven to pasture or market. Back in that time, there were fences in front of every home in any village and stone walls lining both sides of any road—all to keep livestock under control. People were required to wall their property and the walls had to be a certain size and height. It was the Fence Viewer who inspected this and who fined anyone who did not do it right.

The office of Hog Reeve was similar to that of Pound Keeper or Field Driver in that it was this man's job to see that the management of livestock was done in accordance with the law, but the Hog Reeve only tended to (you got it) pigs. See, early on, pigs were allowed to range all over a village but they would eat most anything and any garden was fair sport . . . or any orchard or bush. Pigs made a mess. The Hog Reeve enforced the rule that every pig had to have a yoke around its neck to prevent it from getting through fences. The pig also had to have a piece of wire twisted through the cartilage of its snout in such a way that it would discourage rooting. Apparently this job was beneath the dignity of the Pound Keeper and was a separate office.

After pigs no longer ran free (that is, had to be penned), the election of Hog Reeve continued in many towns as a joke. In Wolfeboro, for instance, for years all the men who had been married between the time of town meeting and the previous town meeting, were lined up in the front of all and unanimously elected as Hog Reeves. There was much hooting and knee slapping when this was done.

See people didn't have television back then.

In Peterborough though, people are more sophisticated than to elect Hog Reeves. For them Fence Viewer is much more sophisticated. ✒

Maude, Mollie and Maggie

BACK AT THE turn of the 20th century, there was a printing and stationery business in Littleton, owned and operated by Eli Wallace.

Back in the 1890s, it was common to see Eli Wallace and his wife, Myra, in their carriage, clopping down Main Street. The rig was pulled by two of the most handsome Morgan horses you could imagine. Maude and Mollie were their names and for 31 years they served their owners. Everyone in town knew Maude and Mollie.

But then the horses got old and infirm and, in 1919, Eli and Myra had them put down, and they were buried side by side in a lovely little cemetery just down the hill from the Littleton Hospital.

Later on, another horse, a mare called "Maggy" was interred there as well. Maggy had pulled the wagon for Littleton's Central Market. Eli knew the horse and was friends with its owner and offered the spot to him in friendship.

Half a dozen years later, Eli's wife passed away and a couple years after that, Eli himself passed on. In his will he stipulated that he would give the hospital forty acres of land that abutted theirs and also a third of his entire estate if they would agree to maintain the cemetery.

Many years later, when Interstate 93 was being improved, it looked as if they would have to move the cemetery but, instead, the road itself was moved. Today the little burying ground is maintained by the trustees of the hospital with the cooperation of the Littleton Historical Society. And thousands of people come every year to see the granite markers of Maude and Mollie and Maggie and to ponder a love that used to be. ❧

First potato

JUST BEYOND A berm in Derry is one of the most important historical sites in America; a site important because of the Conquistadors and Sir Walter Raleigh.

The Conquistadors and Sir Walter Raleigh responsible for some of Derry's town history? You bet!

Here is the chronology:

In 1539, the Conquistadors pillaged Peru. They looted gold and precious gems from the Incas and the Incan graves and carried them back to Europe. They also discovered in the Andes an exotic root plant, which they took home to Spain and cultivated along the Biscay Coast. It was here that Sir Walter Raleigh obtained a few seed roots, which he took to his 40,000-acre plantation outside of Cork in Ireland.

The root was, of course, the potato. The soil of Ireland was perfect for the vegetable.

In 1621, the potato was planted in Jamestown, Virginia. It did not grow.

Then, in 1719, a group of immigrants came to New England. They were lead by a Presbyterian minister, the Reverend James Macgregor. They were Scotsmen who had settled in Londonderry in Northern Ireland. There they experienced persecution from both the Church of England and the Roman Catholics.

They came here from Northern Ireland for religious freedom, and they settled in a place called Nutfield, so-called because of all the walnut and chestnut and oak trees that abounded here. And they established the first Presbyterian congregation in all of North America—and the first potato field in all of North America.

Later on they would change the name of their town from Nutfield to Londonderry and, later still, the town would be divided again into Londonderry, Windham and Derry.

In Derry is the place where the so-called common field for the community was first plowed—and the first potato was grown. ❧

First car in Jaffrey

THE FIRST AUTOMOBILE seen in the United States arrived from France in 1892. It was operated by C.A. Duryea.

It would be a dozen years after that before an automobile would come to Jaffrey. The town history tells us that the first car to be owned here was reported in the *Peterborough Transcript* on June 23, 1904.

"A. M. Butler," the story ran, "is the possessor of a new Ford Automobile of ten horsepower, manufactured by the Ford Motor Company of Detroit, Michigan."

That was the first car . . . but the second would not be far behind. Three weeks later, in fact, the *Transcript* reported that "Asahel Annett has recently purchased a ten-horsepower Cadillac."

Ten horsepower seems to be the norm for 1904.

The *Jaffrey Town History* also has an indication that perception of the new horseless wonder would not change even though years would pass.

With only two cars in town, the *Transcript* noted, "The Selectmen have recently posted notices warning drivers of automobiles not to exceed a speed of eight miles an hour in the village . . . fifteen miles an hour outside."

Plus ça change, plus c'est la même chose. ☙

First shot at Bunker Hill

DEERFIELD IS THE home of John Simpson who was a member of the militia at the Battle of Bunker Hill.

"Don't shoot 'til you see the whites of their eyes," General Israel Putnam is supposed to have said. Actually, the order was, "Don't fire until the word is given."

Simpson was serving under Captain Dearborn. They were part of Colonel John Stark's troops. Anyhow, John Simpson got a British officer perfectly in his sights and couldn't help himself. He fired his musket before the word was given. The shot hit its mark. The officer was brought down. Nevertheless, the next day there was an inquiry and Simpson was arrested and court marshaled.

His punishment, however, was only because his superiors felt that, in light of the fact that he had shot a British officer off his horse, it was a positive outcome.

After the war, John Simpson held the rank of major. He returned to Deerfield and, for the rest of his life, farmed. He never applied for a pension, although he legally was due one. He was quoted as saying, "My country is too poor to pay pensions."

Obviously a patriot and an honest man, but more importantly, John Simpson has the honor of being the first man to fire a shot at the Battle of Bunker Hill. ✒

The troublesome bass violin

THE TOWN OF Brookline once owned a bass violin that caused a lot of trouble. Seems the instrument was used to accompany the choir in the Congregational church. This was back when townspeople were taxed for the church and minister.

The use of a bass violin was common back before churches had organs. The bass viol provided the continuo for the hymns. The sound thrilled the congregation. And that was just the point.

At the Brookline town meeting of 1813, the more conservative Christians argued that the bass violin was simply sinful. It was not godly to feel thrilled in church. The Lord should be praised only with the human voice, they said. Use of musical instruments was sacrilegious because it was suggestive of worldly pleasures; it would lead the congregation into forbidden ways.

The pro-bass violin faction said, "Nonsense. King David himself had played on a harp, and Miriam sang her song of triumph accompanied by the timbrel." (A timbrel, by the way, is a tambourine.) They called the conservatives "old fogies."

In the end, the modernists carried the day. The anti-fiddle people were soundly defeated and the bass violin was used at services for another 25 years when it was replaced by the organ.

No one seems to know where the violin went.

Makes you wonder what those conservative people would have thought of Christian rock 'n roll . . . or Godspell . . . or Jesus Christ Superstar. ◆

The captivity of Mrs. McCoy

THIS HAPPENED THE SUMMER of 1747 in Epsom.

Charles McCoy lived here and he had heard that Indians were camping in the woods at Penacook (now Concord).

So he went to Pembroke and learned it was true: Indians were in the vicinity. He hightailed it for home to take his wife and family to Nottingham where there was a defended garrison and where most of the town had already repaired to.

However, the Indians saw McCoy and followed him home to Epsom. Later, when his wife had been taken prisoner, the Indians told her that they had looked through cracks in the McCoy house that night and had seen what they had for supper. They, however, did not see the McCoys as they were out of their cabin.

The Indians waited overnight to learn how many people were left in the village. The next day was August 21. That morning, Charles McCoy's wife, Isabella, took their two dogs and walked around the settlement to see if any of the other families had returned from the garrison.

She found no one.

On her way back to her cabin, she passed the blockhouse. The blockhouse stood near the present site of the Epsom meetinghouse. Here the dogs began growling. Mrs. McCoy ran for home.

The McCoys now knew that the Indians were in town, and they got ready to go at once to the garrison at Nottingham. Along with Charles and Isabella was their son John—three in all. The younger children were already at the garrison. The McCoys secured their house and set off.

McCoy and his son carried their guns with them, but they had no ammunition. This was because they had been hunting and had fired away all their powder and shot. As they walked, Mrs. McCoy fell behind the men. The Indians now had the opportunity to separate her from her husband and son.

The Indians (three men and a boy) lay in ambush near the foot of Marden's Hill. Here they let McCoy and his son John pass. But, as Isabella came by, they reached from the bushes and grabbed her.

They tried to cover her mouth with their hands, but she was able to scream out.

The men heard her cries and rushed back. The Indians raised their rifles. Isabella knew her husband and son had no ammunition and she yelled at them to run.

They ran.

The Indians then went back to the cabin and collected what booty they could find. This included pots and pans and a trammel, which is an adjustable pot hook which swings over the fire in the fireplace. They also picked some apples from the only tree in town. Then, with their prisoner, they set off for Canada.

They first took Mrs. McCoy to a place near the little Suncook River. Here they left her in the care of the young Indian boy, while the three braves, whose names were Plausawa, Sabatis, and Christi, went away.

Mrs. McCoy later wrote that she thought of attempting an escape. She thought she might kill the Indian boy with the trammel. She was afraid of what was to happen to her—perhaps death or long captivity. But, on the other hand, she didn't know where she was. If she tried to kill her young keeper, she might fail. If she succeeded, she might be caught. That would certainly mean death. So she decided to wait and see.

Soon the Indians returned and put an end to any thought of escape. From the direction in which they had gone and returned, and from their smutty appearance, she guessed they had been burning her house. Plausawa, who could speak some broken English, told her they had.

Then began their journey to Canada. Isabella expected to suffer greatly on the way—and she did, indeed, find the journey fatiguing, and there wasn't much food. But the Indians did not abuse her. They treated her, in fact, with kindness. Turned out the apples they had gathered were saved specifically for her. They gave her one every day. The apples lasted as far as Lake Champlain. She ate the last one as they crossed the lake in their canoes.

And, by the way, back in Epsom, the tree that grew the apples was for years called "Isabella's Tree."

In lots of ways the Indians went out of their way to help Isabella.

Each night the chief, Plausawa, would make a couch of leaves a distance from his own and cover her with his own blanket.

When they came to a river, one of the braves would carry her across on his back. No insult or indecency was ever offered her during the whole time she was with them.

When they reached Quebec, they sold Isabella as a servant to a French family. And that's the story.

At the close of that war, Isabella came home to Epsom. But she had been very comfortable in Canada. Her husband was a man of rough and violent temper, and she is quoted as saying that she never would have thought of attempting the journey back home were it not for the sake of her children. ✎

The New Hampshire man
and the Indian princess

OF COURSE YOU know the story of John Smith and Pocahontas, how the Indian maiden saved the Englishman from death by staying her father's hand as he went to smite the explorer with a tomahawk.

Well, a similar thing happened to a New Hampshire man back in the 18th century. The story is in the *Nelson History*.

The man's name was Samuel Butterfield, and he was one of the original settlers back when the town was called Packersfield.

It was fall and young Sam had traveled to Groton, Mass., to help relatives bring in the crops. While in the field, he and his cousins and friends were attacked by Indians and captured—but not before Sam had killed two of the marauders.

One of the Native Americans he shot was the son of a chief. This brave was reputed to be the bravest and most powerful of the warriors of the Pawtucket Confederation. He also had won in marriage the daughter of the great sachem of the tribe.

The *Nelson History* tells us the maiden "possessed of a loveliness and spirit rivaling the sunshine of a June morning." So I guess she was pretty good-looking.

With the death of their great warrior, the braves vowed revenge. Samuel Butterfield must die, either by whipping or burning alive. How Sam was to die was submitted to the widow of the dead brave. She, in turn, said to the tribe, "If by killing this man you can bring my husband back to life, then choose what horror you please; but, if not, let him be my servant."

And so it was that Samuel Butterfield of Packersfield, New Hampshire, spent the rest of his life as a slave to an Indian princess. And it is said that, in the end, a bond of love existed between the woman and her slave; a love all the sweeter because it had started with hate. ❧

Scalped

THIS STORY TOOK place during the French and Indian Wars, back in the late 1600s.

The protagonist is Mary Brewster.

Mary Brewster was born Mary Slofer in what is now Kittery, Maine. As a young woman, she married the grandson of Elder Brewster of the Plimouth Plantation and Pilgrim fame. The couple settled in Strawbery Banke, what is now Portsmouth.

At the time, there were half a dozen small houses and one large garrison house with its stockade. Here the settlers would take refuge during Indian attacks. These attacks usually came in the late summer or early fall when the crops were harvested. It was then that the settlers were farthest from their shelters and, thus, most vulnerable. Also, at this time, an attack would bring the spoils of the harvest.

Mary was pregnant and at her home when an attack came. She rushed toward the garrison house but was overtaken by the marauders and struck down with a tomahawk. Her skull was split, and she was scalped alive as she lay on the ground. Afterwards, her friends dragged her into the garrison house where she gave birth to a son.

And, strange to say, she recovered.

They fashioned a silver plate as a cover where her scalp had been, and the wound healed, although she wore a wig for the rest of her life.

Mary Brewster had three more sons and lived to be 87 years old. ❧

Silk stockings

THEODORE GOFFE WAS the great-grandson of Squire John Goffe, who built the first mill in Bedford and for whom Goffstown is named.

Around 1790, Theodore Goffe went to Connecticut and married a woman named Anne Griggs and brought her back to Bedford to live in the family homestead. The homestead was near where Macy's department store is nowadays. The Goffes were gentry, and their estate was as grand as any in the area.

Teddy Goffe was an odd duck.

He had a big heart but had little savoir-faire. His nickname was "Ody."

And his wife, because of her Connecticut upbringing, was called 'Old Connecticut.' She was frugal and conscientious and, apparently, not a beauty. Author George Woodbury, who wrote the book, *John Goffe's Mill* said of 'Old Connecticut,' "Glamor was as foreign to her as makeup."

So it seems odd that, later in her life, she announced that she wanted a pair of genuine silk stockings. Yeah, silk stockings. No one seems to know just why she craved this luxury, especially taking into account the fashions for women in the 1830s. Skirts were huge and went to the floor. Only 'Old Connecticut' and God would know if she were wearing silk stockings. And Teddy Goffe . . . well, from his reputation, it seems that if 'Old Connecticut' were to appear wearing only the silk hose, he just might not notice.

Nevertheless, she wanted silk stockings and she knew how to get them.

First, she commissioned one of her servants, on his next trip down river, to cut some mulberry shoots from any trees he might find. And she planted these mulberry trees. (See, 'Old Connecticu' had, if anything, patience.) The trees grew and a few years later she sent a man to Newburyport to purchase silkworms that were brought in from the Orient. Back home she raised the worms in her own back yard feeding them on the mulberry leaves. Soon they were spinning cocoons.

'Old Connecticut' unwound the cocoons and spun the thread herself and knitted a pair of black silk stockings with the initials A.G.G. knit into the top of each stocking.

And she wore 'em, dammit. And felt good. ❧

A Derry eccentric

NEW HAMPSHIRE HAS had its share of eccentrics, some of whom would put William Faulkner and the bunch from Yoknapatawpha County to shame. Derry, for instance, had Dr. Sylvanus Brown.

Sylvanus Brown was born in Massachusetts in 1807, but he was raised on a farm in Derry. In 1827, Sylvanus graduated from Bowdoin College with a degree in medicine. At Bowdoin, he married his college sweetheart, Mary Doane, in a double ceremony. The other groom was his best friend, Samuel Palmer. The second bride was Lydia Pike.

After their wedding, Dr. Sylvanus Brown and Mary moved to Ipswich, Mass. In Ipswich, he got religion.

This was the time of abolition and temperance and women's rights, and Sylvanus espoused them all. In Ipswich, he studied for the ministry and soon was ordained as a preacher in the Free Baptist Church.

In 1840, his dad died. Sylvanus and Mary then moved back to Derry and the family farm. Here he continued to espouse the great causes. He aided the Underground Railroad and doctored to the poor, often free of charge. He never preached in any church.

As a matter of fact, he had come to dislike most formal religions. Over the years, many people witnessed loud arguments between Dr. Brown and members of the town clergy.

Dr. Sylvanus Brown was physically imposing. He was more than six feet tall, weighed over 300 pounds, and had a black, bristling beard.

His in-your-face manner made him a man that many people hid from. But the poor loved him. And his wife loved him. The couple had one son, Samuel, named for his best friend, Samuel Palmer. The son grew to manhood and, one day, went by to visit his father and mother. He found his dad unkempt and, for a change, not talkative. He refused to let his son in the house.

Young Samuel went away but came back a couple days later. He crept into the house. In the bedroom he discovered something horrible: his mother's body. She had been dead for over a week, and the doctor had been sleeping with the corpse. Mary's body was entombed in the East Derry Cemetery. A few days later, the doctor disappeared. His son went to the cemetery and found his father in the tomb cradling the body of his dead wife.

Six months later, Dr. Brown's friend, Samuel Palmer, also died. Dr. Sylvanus Brown did not cradle the dead body of his friend, but he did cradle the live body of his widow. Lydia and Sylvanus were soon married. It is not known what she thought of his shenanigans in the tomb.

Dr. Brown died violently in the fall of 1870. He was driving his carriage on Kilrea Road. Pulling the rig was "Blessed Charley" (all Dr. Brown's horses were "Blessed;" "Blessed Nancy," "Blessed Lucy"). This day, "Blessed Charley" was not going fast enough, so Dr. Brown poked him with his cane. The cane had a nail in the tip.

"Blessed Charley" bucked and Dr. Syvanus Brown, all 370 pounds of him, fell off the seat onto some roadside rocks. The doctor was so heavy that friends had to drag him home on a shed door. Here he died in the arms of another friend, Joe Bean.

He left a lot of money to the town. The income is used to this day. In his will, Dr. Brown stipulated that he be buried in the center of the town common with no marker. The will also stipulated that Mary be exhumed and placed in the same grave at his side and that the caskets face due west.

Problem was the Derry Common was all ledge. So the couple was buried in the cemetery . . . but their grave is unmarked. ✒

A terrible death

THE KIDS CAME to school one day and found something so horrible that, to this day, it is remembered in the *History of Jaffrey*.

The day was June 15, 1825. It was the first day of the summer school session.

The building was the old Tyler Hill one-room schoolhouse that used to be over on the Old Rindge Road. The schoolhouse was typical for its day. It was about 15-by-15 feet with a very low ceiling and an iron stove in the center. The floors slanted from three sides of the room and the windows were high up so as not to distract the students from their studies.

The building was also located beside the river and, in these warmer days, many of the older kids came to school in boats. In the winter, they often skated to school.

But on this day, Hannah Jane Chapman walked to school. Hannah Jane was 12 and the prettiest girl in the school. Her mom was a widow who lived in East Jaffrey and worked in the cotton mill there. Hannah Jane herself would work in the mill when she turned 15, as would all her five brothers and sisters.

Hannah Jane loved school and, as it was the first day, the first to arrive would have the choice of seats in the classroom. Hannah Jane wanted a seat in the back just under the window where it would be cool. So she set off early and, sure enough, when she arrived, no one was there.

The school, of course, was locked; but Hannah Jane knew that the high windows were not locked, and, as it was so early, she went to the woodshed and found a four-foot piece of oak which she dragged across the yard and leaned up against the wall just under the window.

She then climbed the log using it as a ladder and sprung the window which was hinged from the top and tipped in. She pushed her books over the sill and let them drop on the floor and then, holding the window with one hand, tried to push herself over the sill.

But the log was not stable and it tipped. Hannah Jane lost her footing and let go of the window which fell, catching the poor girl right at the neck. And so it was that when the other kids arrived, they found the lifeless body of their friend hanging as if on the gallows.

Today the school is gone. Not even a foundation marks the spot where, many years ago, the prettiest girl in school became the sad victim of her own enthusiasm. ❧

Concord massacre

GEORGE GEERS PHOTOGRAPH

*These stones in the Old North Cemetery remember
those killed in the Concord massacre.*

A GRANITE MONUMENT marks the spot where the worst Indian massacre in the history of Concord occurred.

Here's the story:

It happened in the middle of August in 1746. There had been a lull in the wars between England and France, and many colonists felt safe enough to return to the frontier.

Concord, by the way, was called Rumford back then.

Anyhow, that spring France again declared war on England, and the French and Indian War was with us once again.

The settlers here built a bunch of garrison houses in various parts of the town. One up where North Main Street is now. Another at the South End. One in East Concord, one in West Concord and one in Millville, up near where St. Paul's School is today.

In case of Indian attack, the citizens ran to the nearest garrison house and mounted a defense.

All able-bodied men in town were part of a militia and the settlers had petitioned the Royal Province to send more.

On August 8th, Lieutenant Jonathan Bradley arrived in Rumford with 10 additional militiamen. They were there for the protection of the community.

The next day was Sunday, and all the men of the community took their weapons to church. Indians were seen outside the service by a small girl named Abigail Carter, but there was no trouble.

The next day Lieutenant Bradley and seven other men went out to scout for Indians. In the party were Bradley's brother, Samuel, William Stickney, Alexander Roberts and Obadia Peters. These men all lived in town. There were also three other men, part of the reinforcements sent two days before. These were John Lufkin, John Bean and Daniel Gilman.

The party of eight was coming along when Daniel Gilman saw a hawk up ahead and went to shoot it. The Indians were lying in ambush and let him pass. They wanted to catch the men as a group. As the men approached, one Indian shot at them.

Daniel Gilman turned and saw the ambush. He later said Lieutenant Bradley cried out, "Lord have mercy on me . . . fight!"

Gilman hightailed it out of there and went to the Millville garrison to get help.

In the meantime, the Indians killed four men—Peters, Lufkin, Bean and Lieutenant Bradley's brother, Sam. Stickney and Roberts gave up and were taken prisoner, but Bradley would not yield. He was finally tomahawked to death. All the dead were scalped.

An ox cart from the Millville garrison transported the scalped men into town to Osgood's Tavern, near what is today Depot Street. There they were put on display. All the town turned out to see them. All wept aloud.

The men are buried here in the Old North Cemetery.

We know the story of their brave fight only because prisoner Alexander Roberts managed to escape from his captors and return to Rumford with his tale.

And that is the story of the great Concord massacre. ◞

Flywheel disaster

THE DAMS AT Amoskeag Falls provided the first power to the great mills in Manchester before the steam boilers came. Water power required a steady and strong way to get the power to the machines.

This was done with a flywheel. Now flywheels are big heavy wheels that store energy. You get them spinning and they want to keep spinning, and it requires a lot less power to keep them going.

The mills used these giant wheels first with water power and, later, with steam power. Inside a building right next to the Granite Street Bridge, there was a flywheel that was made of cast iron and weighed 68 tons. It was a full 30 feet in diameter and filled up three stories of the mill. The power from this flywheel served four mills where huge leather belts tied the power into the machines.

Well, on the morning of October 15, 1891, the giant wheel began to wobble and whine as it spun. The bolts and rivets that held the cast iron onto the wheel were coming apart.

The engineer and overseer of the flywheel power station was Samuel J. Bunker. He and his two assistants, Mary Kane and Ada Cram, were alarmed and were attempting to slow the wheel down when the unimaginable happened. The wheel exploded like a land mine, throwing great pieces of iron out through the roof and the brick walls of the mill into the dressmaking machinery and out into the river.

Zebulon Northrop was overseeing some dozen women in the shop when the explosion came. None of the women were injured but the two women assistants and the engineer were killed instantly. ✎

Fitzwilliam's highwayman

IT WAS MARCH 3, 1811. The snow was deep on the turnpike between Marlborough and Fitzwilliam.

Just before sunset, a man rode out of Fitzwilliam on horseback. A mile or so down the road, he passed a sleigh coming the other way. In the sleigh were a Troy man named Luke Harris and a young boy named Charles Tolman.

As they passed, the man on horseback turned around and followed them for a while and then went ahead.

As they came around a corner, they found he had dismounted and was loading a pistol with powder. "Deliver up your money," he cried at the driver. "Deliver up your money or you are a dead man!"

Luke Harris gave the man his pocketbook.

The robber then ordered Harris to turn his sleigh around and return back toward Keene. They complied until they were out of sight. Then Harris turned the horse around again, but the sleigh tipped over.

The two were attempting to right the sled when the highwayman rode up. He was furious that they had not followed his instructions. This time he held a knife to their throats and ordered them to turn around and continue toward Keene. 'Course he had to help right the sleigh first.

The robber then watched them out of sight. They went a couple miles until they came to a house belonging to a man named Tolman Knight. Here they stopped and told their story.

Meanwhile, the highwayman was riding toward Fitzwilliam when he met a man named Willard coming the other way. The man was on foot leading a team of horses. The highwayman drew his pistol just as a man named Powers rode up on horseback. Both men now had their hands in the air. However, between them they had only a few cents. The robber rode off.

Willard, the man with the team of horses, then borrowed Mr. Powers' horse and, following the trail of the robber, rode to the next house on the road, the Osgood family house. As he approached the house, he yelled that there was a highwayman on the loose and they should come out and form a posse.

The front door of the house opened and, instead of one of the Osgood family, the robber himself appeared. As he approached Willard, he drew his gun, but Willard jumped on him from the horse and the two rolled on the ground. The robber pulled a knife, cut Willard's hand, leaped on his horse and rode off. In the scuffle, he lost his hat. The next morning, the entire region was looking for the highwayman.

Dr. Samuel Lane was the first to see him. He was in his buggy when he confronted the robber coming out of the woods. The doctor asked him who he was.

"I am the man . . . I am the man pursued," he said and then pulled out his pistol. "You are a rascal and you are in my power," he said.

But the doctor was too fast and slammed the robber with his horse whip. The robber then tried to stab the doctor, but Doctor Lane grabbed him by the hair. "Murderer!" he hollered.

Just then a man named Jonas Robinson and another named Starky rode up, and the three subdued the culprit.

The highwayman turned out to be a guy named George Ryan. He was a resident of St. Johns, Canada, and he had a serious drinking problem.

And, in fact, on the 10th of May, when he was brought to trial in Charlestown, he pleaded "not guilty" due to drunkenness.

The jury took only a half hour to find him "not guilty." Apparently he was a nice-looking and personable guy when he was sober and, if he had been found guilty, the sentence would have been death.

In the end, he went back to Canada where he, reportedly, lead a quiet life. ✒

Farming out the poor

ABRAHAM LINCOLN SAID that God must have loved the poor because he made so many of them.

Back before Medicare and Medicaid, before county homes, before what we now call public welfare, local towns took care of their paupers by placing them in individual families—much as we care for foster children today.

Back then, say 250 years ago, when a new family arrived in a New England town and before they could settle, it was ascertained if they could support themselves. If it was deemed that they could not, the family was visited by the town constable and warned out of town, that is, told to leave at once.

The townspeople did not want to assume the burden of feeding and housing any person who was not of the town. Nowadays, we do a similar thing when a town zones so as to keep poor people with kids out of their community.

In Fitzwilliam, the town history tells us that back in Colonial times, the constable warned every new family out of town before they even found out of they were solvent. It was considered a prudent action, just in case.

Now that doesn't mean that the citizens were hard-hearted when it came to their own. Far from it. The town history tells us that, in 1785, the wife of a man named Abraham Rice Jr., became ill. The citizens then voted an appropriation of 15 pounds, 10 shillings for her care.

In 1787, the history tells us the town voted "to put out Mr. Putler's family to such persons as should take the care of them at the lowest." That ended up costing the town from six to eight pounds for each person in the family, the history says.

In 1792, the records tell us that one Lt. Daniel Mellen bought old Mr. Camp for one year. He is, the records read, to have two pounds and seven shillings per week, and the said Lt. Mellen is to keep Mr. Camp's clothing as good as when he received him.

This farming out of the poor had advantages, as well as disadvantages, the history says. It should be borne in mind that the pauper went into the family as one of its members and was expected to do such work as he or she was able. The compensation received from the town depended largely on the pauper's ability to labor.

The history also notes, "It is believed that such persons were seldom overworked or misused in Fitzwilliam." ⚬

Smallpox cemetery

IN JAFFREY, UP in the woods above the D.D. Bean Match Co., there is a cemetery that has no gravestones. In fact, there is nothing to indicate that anyone is buried there.

This is the smallpox cemetery.

Buried here are six souls including a 12-year-old girl and a soldier of the Revolutionary War.

All were buried at night by the light of lanterns with no clergy to pray for their souls.

All died horribly in pain and disfigurement. All died of smallpox, in 1792, in a pest house. This is not a pretty story.

In 1792, a smallpox epidemic swept the country. And in Jaffrey, there was a progressive physician named Adonliah Howe. Dr. Howe had read the literature that indicated that if a person could experience a mild form of the disease they would form a resistance to the deadly form.

No one knew about antibodies back then or, for that matter, how to create a serum. It was very crude. A little scratch and a drop or two of water with puss from an infected person would bring on the disease.

Dr. Howe petitioned to have a pest house and wished to experiment with inoculation.

The town went nuts. A petition was circulated. No one wanted such a thing here. But the good doctor had friends in the local government . . . and he was allowed to do his experiment.

The pest house operated from the end of August 'til January, four months. The history does not tell us how many came but it does tell us that six patients did not survive and that they were buried up the hill in an old pasture.

There rest the remains of Eliza Danforth of Amherst, 12-year-old Nancy Thorndike of Jaffrey, 23-year-old Enoch Thurber of Keene, a Mr. Cambridge of Rindge, Oliver Gould of Jaffrey, and a judge, the honorable Abel Wilder of Winchendon. Judge Wilder was a delegate to the National Presidential Convention to be held in Baltimore. Baltimore was the country's center of smallpox contagion and he felt it better to take his chances with inoculation.

The chance he took killed him.

The cemetery has always been shunned and, even today, it is not marked. ✒

Derryfield Beef

MANCHESTER IS HERE, of course, because of the Amoskeag falls. And way before the first Europeans arrived, there were major trails from all over New England leading to the falls.

This was because of the fish.

In the spring millions of fish—especially salmon—came up-river, and at times were so prevalent that a person could scoop the fish up with bare hands. Shad and alewives were easily caught in nets in the pools below the falls.

The first settlers purchased fishing spots at the falls . . . rocks and places on the banks . . . and left these spots to their children and their children's children.

There were all kinds of fish at Amoskeag but the most popular fish caught here were eels. These were the easiest fish of all to catch. You didn't even need a hook and line or a net. You, in fact, could catch 'em by hand in the shallower water.

They were slimy critters but they were delicious and could be salted easily and preserved and sold to the people down in Boston and Portsmouth and Newburyport. They were the town's number one way of making money.

Everyone loved eels.

The city back then was called Derryfield and the eels were referred to by one and all as "Derryfield Beef."

Derryfield Beef was so renowned that General John Stark's grandson, William Stark, even wrote a poem about it. Here's how it reads:

> *Our fathers treasured the slimy prize:*
> *They loved the ell a their very eyes:*
> *And of one 'tis said, with a slander rife.*
> *For a string of ells he sold his wife.*
>
> *From the eels they formed their food in chief*
> *And eels were called "the derryfield beef"*
> *And the marks of eels were so plain to trace*
> *That children looked like eels in the face*

And before they walked it is well confirmed
That the children never walked, but squirmed
So mighty power did the squirmers wield
O'er the goodly men of old Derryfield

That it was often said that their only care,
And their only wish, and their only prayer
For the present world and the world to come
Was a string of eels and a jug of rum! ❧

Cash and carry

THIS STORY IS in L. Ashton Thorp's *History of Manchester*, and Mr. Thorp tells us, "this incident, which seems almost incredible, actually took place."

So it is a true story.

The setting is a grocery and meat market which used to stand in Granite Square, at the corner of Granite and Main Street on the west side of the city.

The sign above the business said "H. Fradd and Company." The "H" stood for the owner, Horatio Fradd, a man of good humor and quick wit.

Inside the store were the goods, but out on the front platform Horatio Fradd kept his barrels of rum and his kegs of sugar.

Well, one day a woman came into the store. She had only recently moved to Manchester and had never before been in the establishment.

And she had never met Horatio before.

The woman asked to purchase 20 pounds of sugar.

Mr. Fradd noted that he did not have 20 pounds of sugar in the store and would have to go outside and open one of the barrels on the platform.

The woman followed him out and said that maybe he would not have to open the barrel after all. She might purchase an entire barrel. And what would a barrel of sugar cost?

Well, Horatio looked at the woman and looked at the large barrel and he wondered how she would get it home, and he said, jokingly, "Heck, if she could carry it home she could have it for nothing."

Ha, ha.

The woman cocked her head and, looking Horatio Fradd right in the eye, took hold of the barrel, swung it up to her shoulder just like she was a stevedore.

She then walked down the stairs and down the avenue all the way to her home on Douglas Street leaving poor Horatio Fradd in a stunned silence, pondering just how expensive a joke he had played on himself. ❧

Epping ghost story

THE GHOST STORY I'm about to tell took place in the town of Epping over a hundred and eighty years ago, in 1820. The story is told in the *New Hampshire Book of Folk Tales*, published back in 1932 by the New Hampshire Federation of Women's Clubs.

Nathaniel Hunter was a young boy who worked on the farm of Squire Daniel W. Ladd in Epping. Nat was friends with, and used to play with, the Cook boys. The Cook boys lived out on Cooks Corner and the Cook boys had a secret: the Baptist Church, they said . . . the one at Simon's Crossing . . . the Baptist Church was haunted.

So after school one day, the three chums crept out to the church to see if they could see a ghost.

They were not disappointed.

As they approached the church they heard a low moaning and a great crashing sound. The hair on the back of their necks stood on end and they went screaming home.

Squire Ladd grabbed Nat as he tried to rush by and Nat told him the story. Now Squire Ladd knew Nat to be a hard-working and, more to the point, a truthful boy. If Nat heard ghosts at the Baptist Church, it was worth a look-see. So the Squire and Nat started back to the church. On the way they picked up General Joseph Towle to come with them.

Sure enough, as the two men and a boy approached the church they heard a mournful sound and a great clanging and creaking from within.

Squire Ladd and General Towle crept up to he door of the church and flung it open. . . .

. . . Sure enough, a dozen non-human eyes looked at them from within the sanctuary and a great lowing was emitted.

You guessed it; the church was filled with cows.

Here's what happened:

Seems that one of the farmers in the neighborhood had turned his cows onto the public roadway to feed. The cows had wandered into the front yard of a lady named Sweetie Cilley.

Sweetie Cilley is described in the history as an eccentric person. Anyhow Sweetie had been so upset that the cows were out that she opened the church door and the cows, thinking it a barn, went in.

The action solved Sweetie's problem but it scared a lot of people. And for quite a few Sundays thereafter the Baptist meeting had a certain aroma.

And nobody talked about ghosts for quite a while. ❧

THE TOWNS

Alstead

THE TOWN OF Alstead is the most northern town in Cheshire County. The first name given this place was a simple number, in this case, Number Four. Seems there were nine forts established in an arc pattern starting in what is now Chesterfield and ending in what is now Lempster. They were called, Number One, Number Two . . . and so on.

By the way, these were not the forts on the Connecticut River that also were called Number One, Number Two, etc.

If you find this confusing, so did the people back then. In fact, in 1752, New Hampshire Colonial Governor Benning Wentworth officially changed the name of Number Four to Newton.

So, then the colony had only one Number Four. That in what is now Charlestown.

There was a problem with this name, too, though. In fact it was the same problem that they had had with the name Number Four. That problem was that now there were also two Newtons.

See, there already was a town called Newton. It is, in fact, still there, down on the border between Plaistow and Hampton.

So Governor Wentworth was a little red-faced and had to find another name pronto. So what he chose to do was name the town after his favorite textbook.

Yeah, you heard me right.

Alstead is named after a textbook. Seems Benning Wentworth

went to Harvard, and at Harvard he ran across a most remarkable book. A book that was something new to the world . . . an encyclopedia published and written by a German scholar, one Johann Heinrich Alstead.

Cotton Mather said of Alstead's encyclopedia, "It held everything that can be learned about man in this life." It even had the first article ever written about the use and abuse of tobacco.

Alstead has, by the way, a spectacularly beautiful library building, the Shedd-Porter Memorial Library. ✒

Amherst

THE NATIVE AMERICANS called this place "Quo-quinnapassakes-sana-na-nag-nog."

I don't know what it means in the Abanaki language that was spoken here then. Something like, "Here we are beside the river." An article in the *Milford Cabinet*, dated 1907, noted that pronouncing the name was like riding on a corduroy road in a wheelbarrow. "Quo-quinnapassakes-sana-na-nag-nog."

The first Europeans to come here called the place "Narragansett Number Three." They were making a map so they could sell the place. They figured the people who called it "Quo-quinnapassakes-sana-na-nag-nog" couldn't possibly own it.

And sell it they did, in 1735. The group came from Salem, Mass., who made a settlement and called the place Souhegan West after the river it abutted. It was a god-forsaken place back then. One settler wrote, "A howling wilderness it was where no man dwelt. The hideous yell of wolves, the shriek of owls, the gobbling of turkeys and the barking of foxes was all the music we heard. All a dreary waste and exposed to a thousand difficulties."

But things got better and, in 1760, the folks who lived here petitioned to become a town and the powers that be gave it the name of the commander-in-chief of the British forces in North America, old Jeffrey Amherst. It was to be the last name change.

Now, Amherst is a nice name, but there are a lot of Amhersts around. Not so many "Quo-quinnapassakes-sana-na-nag-nogs" though. ❧

Legislature first meets

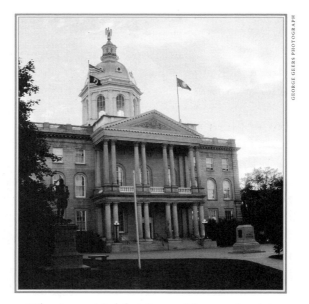

GEORGE GEERS PHOTOGRAPH

*Other towns tried, but Concord became the state
capital because of the fair prices it charged.*

DO YOU KNOW when the legislature first met in Concord?

Many might guess 1818. That's when the original Statehouse was built; but before that, the legislature met other places . . . .

Portsmouth was New Hampshire's first state capital—that was when we were part of Great Britain; Portsmouth, because it was closest to England.

After the Revolution, Exeter was the state capital. But Concord was not the only choice for our Capital City.

In the early 1800s, Hopkinton was in the running to be the state capital. Daniel Webster's hometown of Salisbury also bid for the honor. But Concord won out.

Twice Manchester has tried to take the capital away from Concord, both times when the Capitol building was to be reconstructed and doubled in size. The first was in 1864 in the middle of the Civil War; and the second was in 1909 when the merchants of Manchester offered a million dollars for the state coffers if the capital would relocate.

It goes without saying that, in both instances, the offer was turned down. But that doesn't address my question about when the legislature first met in Concord. It was, in fact, 1781. A Revolutionary Assembly governed us then. The assembly met in Exeter. But when the assembly came to town, the merchants and hustlers doubled their prices for everything. It was a Yankee thing.

But Judge Timothy Walker, who represented Concord, invited the members to hold their next assembly in his hometown. He promised that the food and lodging people there would charge only fair prices. In other words, a lot of money could be saved. The assembly came and had a great time. And that started it all. ✒

New Hampshire's state flower

NEW HAMPSHIRE'S STATE flower is? . . .

That's right, you do know.

New Hampshire's state flower is the *purple lilac*.

But do you know why and when the purple lilac became the state flower? And were there any other choices?

Well, it turns out there were other choices. And up in the legislature there was a huge fight over which flower should become the official state bloom, a fight that makes today's state school funding issue look like a walk in the park.

Hey, people have opinions on everything—but, boy—when it comes to matters of taste, watch out. Suppose, for instance, you could vote on an official state dog. Well, you know that the official New Hampshire state dog should be a . . . a pug! See how you are feeling right now? Who would be stupid enough to even suggest New Hampshire should adopt an official state dog? To do so would only make trouble where there was no trouble before.

Now I gotta say that it was a lot easier for the legislature to adopt an official bird . . . the purple finch . . . . or the official state tree . . . the white birch . . . than it was the state flower.

I'm not sure why, but I think it's because more people have more hands-on experience with flowers than they do with trees or birds.

Now, as I say, the whole thing was a mess from the start. And the start was back in 1919, right at the time they were voting to ratify prohibition. No one's done a study on whether the lack of booze had anything to do with the big brouhaha up in Concord. One thing could be said and that is that even without alcohol, sober minds were not prevailing.

It all started when Rep. Charles Drake, a physician from Lebanon, put in a bill to have the purple lilac designated the New Hampshire state flower. Wow. Right off there were four other bills filed to have the wood lily, the water lily, the golden rod and the pasture rose designated the state flower.

Of the bunch (no pun intended), the water lily got the most publicity because of prohibition. Seems those in favor of banning booze were called the water candidates and a water lily seemed an apt symbol.

Besides, they said, the purple lilac was not indigenous to America. It was imported from Bavaria.

So what, said the proponents of the purple lilac. The first flower planted at Governor Wentworth's mansion in Portsmouth was the lilac. It is, in fact, the oldest imported plant in New Hampshire.

All five bills championing each flower were referred to the House Agriculture Committee. And they made a choice: the apple blossom!

What a mess.

All six bills were immediately killed in committee. Too controversial. Yeah, but the idea had been planted (again no pun intended). Rep. Charles Peterson of Plainfield demanded a showdown between the purple lilac and the apple blossom. "OK," the members said, and voted for the apple blossom. So a bill was sent to the state Senate.

In the meantime, a bill recommending the mayflower was voted down in the House. In the New Hampshire Senate the buttercup was suggested . . . big fight. So big, in fact, that they decided finally to put the flowers in a hat and decide by draw.

So they put the names of the purple lilac and the mayflower and as someone insisted, the purple aster, in a hat and drew. . . . You guessed it. The winner was the purple aster!

The House was livid. How dare they send the purple aster for their consideration; it hadn't even been discussed in the House.

Off it went to conference committee, where, sure enough, it was deadlocked. Again they decided to let George do it . . . that is, not make a decision themselves . . . and they sent it off to two botanists, one at Dartmouth and the other at UNH (which was more of an aggie school and was called the New Hampshire College back then).

The two botanists were in complete agreement with the legislature—that is, they couldn't agree either. Professor Orman Butler of Durham said the state flower should be the evening primrose—certainly not the purple lilac! Professor Arthur Chivers of Dartmouth said, no doubt about it, the state should choose the purple lilac.

It went back to a House committee, and the committee said, a pox on both your opinions, we stand behind . . . the purple aster.

So how did the purple lilac get to be the state flower? Simple, as usual. It was power.

A joint conference committee was appointed and told to get this matter over with before someone got shot. They huddled and voted, 8 to 2, for the lilac (the other two votes were for the apple blossom) and the bill went through slicker than heck.

And the purple lilac prevailed.

And that's the story.

Now—and I'm not kidding here—we ought to have a state dog. Get in touch with your state rep and vote for the pug.

The pug would make a great state dog. ❧

The New Hampshire state seal

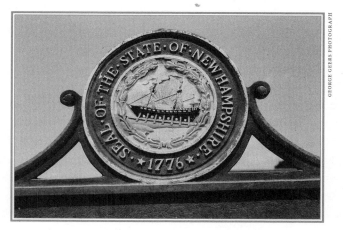

GEORGE GEERS PHOTOGRAPH

The state seal graces the top of the green historical markers you see across the state.

THE NEW HAMPSHIRE state seal has always bothered me. Even as a kid it didn't look right to me.

It's because the ship on the state seal is tipped. Of course it's supposed to be tipped. It is, after all, a ship in dry dock as it were; in "the stocks" the shipbuilders call it. If the ship weren't tipped, it couldn't be launched.

Look at the seal closely and it makes sense. But, at a distance you don't see the horizon; you see only the ship and it looks crooked. "At a distance" is the way most people see it, too, because the state seal is also the state flag.

It looked crooked to me as a kid and it still looks crooked.

The ship, by the way, is the sloop *Raleigh*. It was the first ship completed during the American Revolution. The founding fathers down in Philadelphia sent out a panic directive to have a number of warships built and the first one to be completed with its rigging was the *Raleigh*. The shipbuilders at the Portsmouth Navy Yard worked day and night to complete the job.

The ship sailed off to France accompanied by another American ship, the *Alfred*, to get additional cannon and gunpowder and more crewmen.

On the way, the ships encountered a British man-o-war, the *Nancy*. The *Raleigh* hit it broadside with what cannon it carried. Due to a wind change, the crew was unable to board the British ship but reported that they left it disabled.

History was made that day. It was the first time a battle had been fought beneath Betsy Ross's new *Stars and Stripes* flag.

A month later, on their way back from France, the two American ships went up against two more British ships. This time the British captured the *Alfred*. Captain Thomas Thompson decided that the cause was lost and, instead of coming to the aid of its sister ship, sailed away. Captain Thompson's reasoning was that it was better to save one ship than to do something foolhardy.

Back in Boston, they didn't see things that way, and the good captain was court-martialed.

A new captain took over and soon found himself also in a battle with the British off the coast of Maine. The crew fought valiantly but, in the end, 25 of the men were either killed or wounded. The upshot was that the British took over the *Raleigh* and from then on the ship fought against the colonies.

The British, by the way, loved the ship. She was fast and sailed beautifully. And they used it to capture many American ships, including—at a battle in Charleston Harbor—John Paul Jones' ship, the *Ranger* that had also been built at the Portsmouth Navy Yard.

Now let's get back to the state seal . . .

The original seal featured a codfish and a pine tree on either side of a bundle of five arrows. This signified the two great products of New Hampshire: lumber and fishing, and the five original counties of the state.

In 1784, the seal as we know it was adopted by the legislature. It featured the *Raleigh* in dry-dock with the rising sun behind it and lumber in the foreground.

Over the years the seal kept these features. But, as it was a seal, it was used all the time and wore out a number of times and had to be re-engraved. The engravers took all sorts of liberties with the design over the years . . . until 1931 when the legislature adopted the seal as we see it today. At that time, they also abandoned Latin for English in the inscription surrounding the seal.

And thus it has been since.

But, I don't know. It still looks cockeyed from a distance.

New Hampshire has the shortest coastline of any coastal state in the Union and, yet, our state flag has a nautical theme.

The stylized rising sun in the background looks like a Japanese flag. The ship it shows ran away from one battle and later was captured to become a weapon of the enemy.

And finally, I don't know if you've noticed, but the entire scene is not even in New Hampshire . . . it's in Maine, for gosh sakes. The Portsmouth Naval Ship Yard is in Maine.

We are the only state in the union whose flag features a scene from a neighboring state.

Hey, is this a great country or what? ☙

Congress Street

BACK WHEN WE were a colony of Great Britain, Portsmouth was the capital of New Hampshire. And the Statehouse used to sit in Market Square. The old, two-story wooden building, in fact, sat out where the street is nowadays.

There was a narrow street on one side and an extremely narrow street between the back of the Statehouse and the front of the church on the other. (Actually there was another church, but it sat in, generally, the same place.)

Feeling for independence was high in Portsmouth. After all, these were people who were being taxed by England. And these were among the first to refuse to pay taxes.

So there was a great crowd around the Statehouse on the day that the first copy of the Declaration of Independence arrived in town. On what was then King Street hundreds stood and heard the first reading of the document.

Imagine hearing, for the first time: "When in the course of human events, it becomes necessary for one people to dissolve the political bands which have connected them with another . . . "

And so it was at the end, to hear the words:

"And for the support of this Declaration, with a firm reliance on the protection of divine Providence, we mutually pledge to each other our Lives, our Fortunes, and our sacred Honor."

At that there was a great "hurrah" from the crowd and people threw their hats in the air and a man named Thomas Manning stepped forward there in the middle of King Street and cried:

"And huzza for . . . Congress Street!"

From that moment on, King Street's name was forever changed. To this day it is called Congress Street.

How about that?

Nobody says, "huzza" anymore. ❧

Cowbell Corner

"SHODDY." IT'S AN adjective that means "inferior . . . or made of cheap quality." But do you know where the word itself came from?

It came from a product that was once made right here in Salem, New Hampshire.

"Shoddy" was the name given woolen cloth that was made, not directly from the fleece of sheep, but rather from old woolen cloth and felt. They'd boil rags down and remake fabric from them.

Some of this fabric wasn't too bad, but most of it was inferior to fabric made directly from sheep's wool. It was, in other words, "shoddy."

There used to be a mill right here. It was called, "The N.H. Paul Company" and it made "shoddy" here for 10 years . . . from the end of the Civil War, 1865, to 1875. Before that, there had been a grist mill on the same site.

A photograph of the shoddy mill is in the *Salem Town History*. In the bell tower you can just barely see a small bell there, a bell which gave this section of town its romantic name.

This part of Salem is "Cowbell Corner."

For years I have seen this place on the maps and wondered about it. Was it, at one time, the dairy part of the town? It certainly would bring to mind strapping, healthy milkmaids going about their chores. Oh, how I would dream about the quintessential farmers' daughters.

Well, my dreams have turned to disillusion because, it turns out, the name "Cowbell Corner" has nothing whatever to do with the dairy business. It has, in fact, only to do with the shoddy business.

See, the name is apparently humorous. It was chosen not because there were cows here, but rather because the mill owner was so cheap that he would only invest in a very small bell to call his workers to their labors. So small a bell, in fact, that people took to calling it a cowbell.

Ergo, "Cowbell Corner."

So, the mill made shoddy . . . and it had a shoddy bell. ❧

Exeter

THIS PLACE WAS originally called Squamscott. It was settled and managed first in 1638 by a group of Englishmen known as the Exeter Combination.

The Reverend John Wheelwright was the head of the combination, and it was he who changed the name from Squamscott to Exeter.

Back then, the town encompassed an area of what is now Brentwood, Newmarket and Epping, as well as Exeter.

Exeter in England, where the Reverend Wheelwright came from, is in Devonshire in the southwest of the country. The English town got its name from the River Exe that runs through it.

The River Squamscott runs through Exeter, New Hampshire.

Because of its location on the river, the town used to have a lot of shipbuilding and trading, especially with the West Indies.

Like Portsmouth, Exeter is part of Rockingham County and is its county seat. Rockingham was named in 1769 for a cousin of Colonial Governor Benning Wentworth, one Charles Watson-Wentworth, who was (and this is it) the Marquis of Rockingham.

Exeter, by the way, is one of the few towns in New Hampshire never to be officially incorporated. It's that old.

Before and during the American Revolution, Exeter was the capital of the province and later the state. It was here that the first legislature met, and it was here that the New Hampshire Constitution was adopted, not incidentally, the first state to adopt a constitution.

The town is famous for Phillips Exeter Academy, perhaps the finest prep school in the country.

Native sons include sculptor Daniel Chester French, who carved the Minute Man in Lexington and the Lincoln Memorial in Washington, D.C.

And my favorite native son is Judge Henry Shute, whom my grandfather knew very well. Judge Shute wrote the book *The Real Diary of a Real Boy*, a boyhood reminiscence which Walter Cronkite says is better than Mark Twain. ◗

Henniker

THIS PLACE WAS first called simply, "Number Six." That was back in the 1600s. It was called "Number Six" because it was the sixth of a dozen or so towns linked to each other going from the Seacoast, across the state, and ending at the Connecticut River.

Later, some people came up from Marlborough, Mass., and settled here. They named this place, "New Marlborough."

Then, in 1752, this land was granted to a guy named Andrew Todd. He got a bunch of people to settle here from Londonderry, Chester, Hopkinton and Bedford. They named their town, "Todd's Town."

And so it was called, until 1768, when the citizens begged New Hampshire Governor Benning Wentworth to grant their petition to become an official town.

Governor Wentworth granted their request but changed the name of the town to that of a dear friend of his from England. This was a man who had opened trade between Britain and Russia. He had made a killing and had been knighted.

He was a man who also engaged in trading what were called West Indian goods, that is, rum, sugar and slaves, traded with America for furs, lumber, potash, turpentine and sperm oil. That's how he came to know Benning Wentworth, because that's how Wentworth himself got rich.

Benning Wentworth's friend was Sir John Henniker.

He never saw this place but was, no doubt, pleased that his friend Wentworth had honored him so. And, of course, very few people know anything about Sir John.

But the town of Henniker is famous for being the site of New England College, for being the birthplace of composer Amy Beach, for having the grave site of Ocean Born Mary . . . the baseball player Ted Williams once lived here, as did the poet Edna Dean Proctor . . . and the educator James Patterson.

And, finally, it is known for being the only place in the world called, "Henniker." ❧

Amy Beach

SHE WAS BORN in Henniker just after the Civil War . . . in 1867.

Her folks named her Amy, Amy Cheney.

Amy's daddy was a paper manufacturer. The Cheney family was well-off.

Her mom was a classical singer, a soprano, and also played the piano. It was from her mom Amy got her talent.

When she was only a year old Amy could sing entire songs in tune and, before she turned two, she could harmonize with her mother in duets.

Her mom taught Amy to identify various musical keys by color. For instance, Amy would ask her mother to play "the pink song" or "the green song."

You couldn't, of course, keep a child like this from the piano and by the time she was four, Amy could play Beethoven and even transcribe pieces. By the time she was seven, Amy was performing publicly at charitable events and soirees. When Amy turned eight, the family moved to Boston and enrolled their prodigy daughter in private school where she studied piano.

She made her formal debut as a pianist at sixteen and the next year was featured with the Boston Symphony Orchestra.

By this time, Amy had grown into a very sweet, attractive young woman. She was about five foot five and, as one newspaper described her, "round and rosy." She had a lovely complexion and stunning violet-blue eyes.

She was, as you might imagine, quite serious in her demeanor, but she had a robust and infectious laugh and a great sense of humor.

You also can imagine that she was more comfortable with adults than with kids of her own age.

It came as no surprise then, when in 1885, Amy Cheney fell in love with an older man. Harry Harris Aubry Beach was a prominent Boston surgeon.

When the couple married, Amy was 18. Dr. Beach was 42. It was an overly formal relationship. Dr. Beach had position and repute and was a typical Victorian. He insisted this wife give up her performing career except, of course, for charity.

And she, of course, took the doctor's name. Henceforth, she was known as Mrs. H.H.A. Beach.

Amy Beach was not phased by her new position. Harry Beach was not unlike her own father. Her own mother had been a talented amateur who had traded fame for security. It was the way of the time.

But Amy had this huge talent that would not be bottled up. And, although she had no formal training in composition, she began to compose. Piano pieces at first.

And she was good.

By the time she turned 22, she had completed a grand mass. Three years later, the Handel and Hayden Society presented the hour-long mass to the acclaim of the Boston critics.

Her next triumph was an entire symphony. Her first and, in fact, the first symphony ever composed by an American woman. It was entitled the Gaelic Symphony. Over the years, Amy Beach was to compose 150 different musical pieces. And all but a few were published.

In 1910, Harry Beach died and a couple months later Amy's beloved mom passed away. Amy went back to performing. She was forty two. She then went to Europe and was soloist there with a number of orchestras.

When World War I broke out, she came home to New York City and it was about this time she found the MacDowell Colony in Peterborough.

For 25 years, she came each summer to Peterborough where she composed and wrote letters to conductors urging them to perform her work. Like Marian MacDowell, the founder of the Colony, Amy Beach also had musical clubs all over America. These ladies' organizations were dedicated to the performance of her work.

By the time of her death in 1944, Amy Beach's music had lost favor with the critics. Too sentimental, they said. But nowadays Amy Beach is performed all over the world and she is considered one of the country's great romantic composers.

It is very nice, very listenable, music.

Pretty good for a little girl from Henniker. ✒

Edna Dean Proctor

AMY BEACH WAS not the only famous woman to hail from Henniker. Back in the 19th century there was another female artist who came from here and who also had a national reputation.

This was the poet, Edna Dean Proctor.

Miss Proctor was born in this town on October 10, 1829. She got her primary and secondary education over in Concord but moved early in her adult life to Brooklyn, New York.

Nonetheless she often came back to the Granite State and, if asked, would say New Hampshire was her greatest love.

Her first volume of poems was published in 1869 when she was 31. The work received great acclaim and secured her position among the first rank of American poets.

Ms. Proctor also wrote travelogs which still may be read online.

She traveled most of Europe, Syria, and ascended the Nile. Her best-known book was entitled *A Russian Journey.*

She is also known for her edited extracts from the sermons of Henry Ward Beecher.

Her two best-known poems are entitled "Heroes" and "By the Shenandoah." She also wrote dozens of poems about New Hampshire, including verse to Mt. Kearsarge, the Contoocook River, Mt. Monadnock, and Mt. Washington. My favorite of her verse is one entitled simply, "New Hampshire." This poem was written for the New Hampshire Historical Society on the occasion of the state's bicentennial in 1873.

This is the opening stanza:

"A goodly realm!" said Captain Smith,
Scanning the coast by the Isles of Shoals,
While the wind blew fair, as in Indian myth
Blows the breeze from the Land of Soul
Blew from the marshes of Hampton spread
Level and green that summer day,
And over the brow of Great Boar's Head,
From the pines that stretched to the west away;

And sunset died on the rippling sea,
Ere to the south with the wind sailed he,
But he told the story in London streets,
And again to the court, and prince, and king;
"A truce!" men cried, "to Virginia heats;
The North is the land of hope and spring!"
And in sixteen hundred and twenty-three.
For Dover meadows and Portsmouth River,
Bold and earnest they crossed the sea,
And the realm was theirs and ours forever!

Pretty robust stuff, I think. It stands up pretty good.

Edna Dean Proctor, by the way, died in Brooklyn in 1923. She was 85 years old. ☙

Hillsboro

ONE OF MY favorite villages in all of New Hampshire is Hillsboro Center.

Ever notice how many drop-dead gorgeous towns start with the letter "H"? . . . Hancock . . . Harrisville . . . Hanover . . . Hampton Falls . . . Haverhill . . . Hopkinton . . . Hillsboro Center . . .

All these places that have the word "center" indicate where the town was founded. Most were centered on a high meadow so that after church or a town meeting, it was a downhill walk for the horses.

Later, of course, most towns developed around the waterpower, as it is in the case of Hillsboro. The same is true of Wilton or Jaffrey or a hundred other towns in the state.

Hillsboro, by the way, didn't get its name because it is atop a hill. It *is* on top of a hill, though. I say that although I am not sure how the town got its name.

One theory is the name came from one of the original grantees of this land around there, a guy named Colonel John Hill. Colonel Hill lived in Portsmouth and was a personal friend of Massachusetts Royal Governor John Belcher . . . see, this was back in the 1700s, when Massachusetts controlled New Hampshire. Belcher is the guy for which Belchertown, Mass., is named and also was the founder of Princeton College.

But the fact was that when the new province of New Hampshire was formed, this place was officially named Hillsboro by the then Royal Governor of New Hampshire, Benning Wentworth . . . and he stated that he was naming the place, not after his fellow Portsmouth citizen, Colonel Hill, but rather after an Englishman named Wills Hill.

Wills Hill was the Earl of Hillsboro in England and a member of the king's privy council. He was also president of the board of trade for all the American colonies. That made him an important contact for Benning Wentworth because the governor was getting rich with the trade, and flattering a superior was all the rage . . . then as now.

And, by the way, although Benning Wentworth took the grant in Hillsboro away from the guy named Hill in Portsmouth, he gave him a lot of land in the surrounding towns to compensate his loss, and so everyone seems to have come out of the deal happy.

The county, of course, is also named Hillsborough, in honor of the Earl of Hillsboro, but this town, in effect, got the same name twice from two different guys. . . . It is pretty, though. ❧

Hillsboro bridges

GEORGE GEERS PHOTOGRAPH

The twin-arch bridge on the Antrim/Stoddard is worth a visit.

ON THE ANTRIM/STODDARD town line, by Route 9, is a twin-arch bridge built back in the 18th century by Scotch/Irish settlers.

This area and, specifically Hillsboro, is peppered with stone-arch bridges built by these men. Most of the spans are dry, that is, without mortar. It is just the weight of the stone that holds them up.

This bridge is the easiest one to find and it is worth stopping here to see it, especially during foliage season for a photo opportunity, just to see how beautiful it is. In Hillsboro, the Beard Brook meanders around for about 29 miles and where it goes under Gleason Falls Road, it comes through in two parts: this arch and another that's down about 100 feet spanning the falls on Beard Road . . .

This is the biggest and most impressive stone-arch bridge in Hillsboro. It's been here forever, and it was only replaced a few years ago by another bridge. It's located at the junction of Route 9 and Route 202. I've come across that bridge literally thousands of times in my lifetime.

But my favorite stone-arch bridge in Hillsboro is over the Beard Brook on Jones road. This bridge is fully intact with original granite guard posts. And this bridge has a history. It was the idea of a man who lived just up the road from here, a man named Captain Nathaniel Carr. He needed a good bridge to get home and so he hired the workmen to create this wonderful structure.

What makes this story so interesting is that Captain Carr paid off the workers with money they think he made himself on a printing press he owned. Captain Carr was an imperious man. He was handsome and tall and broad-shouldered. The ladies loved him and the men did his bidding.

He was tried for counterfeiting and found guilty. At his sentencing the judge ordered him to bow his head.

The captain refused. "God Almighty made me to look a man in the face!" he said to the judge. And the judge said back to him, "Ten years!" Which he served. But he never talked.

They found more counterfeit money in a cave up the road and a lot more in his house, but the plates were never found, and Captain Carr went to his grave with the secret of where they were or if anyone helped him in his crime. ☙

Hitty-Titty Pond

SO I'M LOOKING through this old atlas that my grandfather once owned. It dates from 1892. My grandfather, incidentally, was 30 years old in 1892.

But that being neither here nor there, I was looking in the atlas at the town of Salem because I knew I was coming here to do some stories. I was reading the *Town History*, and this atlas is a perfect companion to the old town histories, because it has most of the old names and places.

So I am looking at the map of Salem and of Canobie Lake when I look to the north where Route 111 nowadays comes down by Shadow Lake, and I discover this.

"Shadow Lake" is not called "Shadow Lake" on the old map, it is rather called, "Hitty-Titty Pond."

"What a wonderfully romantic name," I think. "Where did the name ever come from?" I think, "and why did they ever change it?"

So I go to the *Salem Town History* and, on page 25, we find something of its history but nothing of its etymology other than it is a Native American name. But it does not tell us what it meant in the Algonquin language, simply that the Indians called it, "Hitty-Titty." The town history says that "It has lately been corrupted into 'Hit-a-tit' and 'Hit-Tit' without any reasonable justification so far as we can ascertain."

The history goes on to say, "More recently the name Shadow Lake has been applied to it, but the old name still holds sway."

Originally, when all this area was a part of Methuen, Mass., it had been called, "Sachwell's Pond," but for over a hundred years, between 1804 and 1907, this was "Hitty-Titty Pond."

And I, for one, think they should go back to the old name. I mean, "Shadow Lake" sounds like "Yuppieville, USA." No, I think the name should be changed back . . . to "Sachwell's Pond" . . . of course. ✎

Isles of Shoals

THE ISLES OF Shoals sit off the New Hampshire and Maine coast with a name as romantic as any place on earth.

This was the first land sighted by Europeans in the place we now call New Hampshire.

Now you may argue that the first European to see New Hampshire was probably a Viking. There are what some people consider runes (that is, Nordic writing), over in Hampton. And that may be true. But the first *recorded* sighting of what is now New Hampshire was made by Samuel de Champlain.

Champlain is the guy that Lake Champlain is named for.

He sailed past the Isles of Shoals in 1605 and put to shore at Odiorne's Point. He named Odiorne's Point, "The Cape of the Islands." Much good it did him.

It took another nine years before anyone else recorded that they had seen this land. And the next guy to see the islands was Captain John Smith (yeah, the guy "Pocahontas" is supposed to have saved).

It was 1614 when he sailed by the islands. And, I gotta tell you, Captain Smith was impressed. Everywhere he looked around the islands he saw fish, shoals and shoals of them.

See, back then, they called schools of fish "shoals" of fish. Later on they called the shallows where the fish spawned, "shoals," so a lot of people think that the Isles of Shoals means "islands that have a lot of shallows around them."

But Smith meant these were the islands with a lot of fish around them. He wrote, "It was the strangest fish pond I ever saw."

He was so taken by the islands he called them after himself, "Smith's Isles." And the written report that he brought back to England so impressed Prince Charles that the prince named the whole coast and region, "New England."

And so it has been called ever since.

But they didn't call the islands "Smith's Isles" and I, for one, am glad.

"The Isles of Shoals" is much more romantic. ❧

Keene

THE PEQUOT INDIAN tribe inhabited the area that is now western Connecticut. The area was called Ashuelot. North of that area, where Keene is now, was called Upper Ashuelot.

In the early 1700s, Massachusetts awarded this area to militiamen for their service in Canada during the French and Indian Wars.

Colonel Benjamin Bellows was the surveyor of Keene and of most of the towns around. Colonel Bellows went on to found Walpole, and is the man for whom Bellows Falls is named.

The area, like Peterborough and Antrim, was settled and then abandoned during the Indian wars but re-settled by the mid-1700s.

Two hundred and fifty years ago some two dozen men petitioned Governor Benning Wentworth and his council asking to incorporate. It took three years but, finally, the governor acceded to the request. And Governor Wentworth asserted his prerogative to choose a name for the new town.

The name he chose was Keene; chosen to honor his close friend Sir Benjamin Keene.

Who was this Benjamin Keene?

Well, that he was an English peer went without saying. He was also very popular in Britain. Horace Walpole called him, "One of the best kind of agreeable men. Quite fat and agreeable. And easy with universal knowledge."

The writer Horace Walpole, by the way, was the son of England's first prime minister, Sir Robert Walpole, for whom, not incidentally, Walpole, New Hampshire, is named.

Anyhow, Sir Benjamin had once befriended Benning Wentworth when Benning had been cheated in a timber sale in Spain, and Sir Ben was the English minister there.

Wentworth and Keene also did business together. Both were in the business of selling West Indian goods, that is, lumber, rum and slaves.

And so Keene became Keene.

In 1873, it incorporated as a city. It is today the seat of Cheshire County and one of the foremost manufacturing cities in the state. ✎

Milford

FOR MUCH OF its length, the Souhegan River is quite deep.

Today we have a bridge to cross the river, but back before the Europeans discovered this land, the Native Americans who lived there would cross the Souhegan just below a natural fall where the river widened out and became quite shallow.

In the 19th century, they built a granite dam which you can still see. The water behind the dam covers where the ford used to be. Generally, it started where the bridge abutment is today and ran diagonally over toward a group of buildings. And, by the way, my great-grandfather Addison Wetherbee built the second building.

When the first white settlers came here, this area was known as Monson. The name came from the British Lord of Trade, Sir John Monson, who was a personal friend of New Hampshire Colonial Governor Benning Wentworth. People called this part of Monson "The Falls" or "The Mile Slip."

In 1741, a man named John Shepard built a sawmill using the natural falls to power his operation. From then on, this place was called the ford at the mill or the mill ford. Later the settlement that grew up around it was called The Mill Ford Village; hence the name of the town, Milford. ✒

The Caroline Cutter grave

At the tombstone of Caroline Cutter in Milford.

IN THE ELM Street Cemetery in Milford, some of the original set-tlers of the town rest. Many are relatives of mine . . . for instance, the Burns. But, by far the most interesting stone in this yard says,

CAROLINE H.
Wife of
Calvin Cutter, MD
Murdered by the Baptist Ministry of Baptist Church as follows:
Sept 28, 1838, AE 33, she was accused of Lying in Church Meeting by
the Rev. D.D. Pratt of Deacon Albert Adams. Was condemned by the
church unheard. She was reduced to poverty by Deacon William Wal-
lace. When an exparte council was asked of the Milford Baptist Church
by the advice of their committee, George Raymond, Calvin Averill and
Andrew Hutchinson, they voted not to receive any communication upon
the subject: The Rev. Mark Carpenter said he thought as the good old
Deac. Pearson said, "we have got Cutter down and it is best to keep him
down." The intentional and malicious destruction of her character
and happiness as above described destroyed her life.
Her last words were, "tell the truth."

What the heck is going on here? A woman murdered by the Baptist Church? Impossible! And what is this; this fieldstone set right in the middle of this poor woman's grave? This stone is so close to the other as to make the original difficult to read. Is this stone a monument to Caroline, too? No. In fact, this is a monument to her daughter, Carrie, who was the first woman to die in the Civil War.

Again, what's going on?

Well, let me tell you the first part of the story.

The main player in this tale is this guy, "Calvin Cutter, MD." Dr Cutter and his wife lived originally in Nashua and they were fervent Baptists. They loved the church.

However, back before the Civil War, the only Baptist Church in Nashua was up on the heights. Dr. Cutter and his wife and daughter Eliza lived in the south end of town. So did 33 other parishioners. Well, Dr. Cutter and some of the others wanted their own church closer to home and they set about raising money for it.

Now this guy Cutter was a piece of work.

He was one of those guys who, it seemed, was never wrong. Many found him insufferable. And even though few had agreed to fund the new church, he told the builders to go ahead and he'd see it was paid for.

Well, the church was built for thirty-three thousand dollars. But the builders were not paid . . . and Dr. Cutter and his wife were reduced to poverty and had to move out of town.

They came to Milford, where they moved in with his wife's parents, the Halls, on their farm out on the North River Road.

The Cutters then began to attend the Milford Baptist Church on South Street, and Dr. Cutter took to standing up at the end of the services and telling the congregation that, as good Christians, they should donate money to help pay for the Nashua Church. He also took to confronting the members of the parish individually.

The upshot was that he was told he could not attend Milford Baptist services any more.

Dr. Cutter was livid. But the most hurtful thing to happen was that his wife, Caroline, was denounced in church, as well, and told she was not welcome at meetings.

It broke her heart. She stayed home on Sundays and cried and cried and blamed the members of the Church for her misery, not her husband. The daughter, Eliza died, and Caroline became pregnant again. In July, she gave birth to a second daughter, whom they named Carrie. But Caroline never recovered after the birth and, less than a month later, she died.

Dr. Cutter knew it wasn't his fault, it was the fault of the deacons of the church and he was going to get his revenge.

And so he commissioned this stone and announced in the *Farmer's Cabinet* newspaper that it would be erected on a Saturday afternoon here in the Elm Street Cemetery.

That Saturday, hundreds of people milled around waiting for the gravestone but it took the carver longer than he had estimated. It was after midnight before it was put in place.

The next day, after church, a thousand people came by to see the tombstone and to cluck their disapproval. Nobody had the nerve to take it down, and here it has been ever since.

Cutter went off to Massachusetts, re-married and went on the lecture circuit teaching medicine. Later, when the Civil War broke out he enlisted as a surgeon.

And this is when the story of this stone begins. But that's another story. ☙

Cutter gravestones

THE STONE TELLS us that Mrs. Cutter was accused of lying by members of the congregation and, as a result of her excommunication, she died of a broken heart.

What is not said here is that it was her husband, Dr. Calvin Cutter, who, because of his arrogance, was responsible for most of the family's misery.

Anyhow, here lies the first Mrs. Cutter, with her stone proclaiming her "murdered by the Baptist Church."

But now what is this? Here right in front of the stone, and right in the middle of Caroline's grave, is another stone. This monument commemorates the first woman to die in the Civil War. Her name was Carrie Cutter and, yes, Carrie is Caroline's daughter.

Here's how it all happened:

After Dr. Cutter buried his wife, he and his infant daughter moved out of Milford . . . went down to Warren, Massachusetts, a small town east of Springfield. Here Dr. Cutter married again. His second wife was the daughter of one of the town's leading citizens and owner of the mills. Her name was Eunice Powers and she was, to all accounts, his equal. She had been a preceptor in a seminary where Dr. Cutter had lectured.

It was an interesting marriage. Both were ardent emancipationists. At one time, Dr. Cutter tried smuggling guns into Kansas and was nearly killed by ruffians. Later he and his wife tried again to smuggle guns to the anti-slavery forces in Kansas, and again were thwarted by the same ruffians who, this time, considered killing Dr. Cutter but were dissuaded by his wife. She must have been something.

And, by the way, the new Mrs. Cutter and her stepdaughter, Carrie, grew to be great friends and, more importantly, allies. Carrie grew into a beautiful young woman. She had intelligence and grace. She was educated at a private school in Lancaster, Massachusetts, and at Mt. Holyoke Seminary and at a private German school in Pennsylvania.

When the Civil War broke out, Dr. Cutter enlisted as a surgeon in the 21st Massachusetts Volunteers. He was assigned to a hospital ship, the *Northerner*, which sailed with the Burnside Expedition. Carrie was also aboard the ship when it sailed out of Annapolis. She had volunteered as a nurse.

After the battle of Roanoke, Carrie tended the sick and wounded. Because of her ability to speak German, she took care of three young German soldiers with yellow fever who, in their delirium, had forgotten the English language.

But, then, Carrie, too, caught yellow fever. On March 24, 1862, she died in the cabin of the *Northerner*. She was not yet 20 years old. Carrie Cutter was the first woman to die in the Civil War.

General Burnside ordered her to be buried with the full military honors usually accorded the burial of a colonel. Later, when the national cemetery was established at New Berne, North Carolina, her remains were interred there.

Her name is inscribed here in Milford and also on the soldiers' monument in Warren, Mass., that says, poetically, "she sleeps where the magnolia blooms, and overhanging vines bend down and kiss her southern grave."

And that's the usual story about Carrie Cutter, first woman to die in the Civil War and whose mother's grave states that she was killed by the Baptist Church.

But there may be another story, too, for the New Berne Cemetery website tells us this:

". . . she was the sweetheart of Charles E. Coledge, a private of the 25th Massachusetts Regiment, who was very ill with yellow fever. Despite her efforts to care for Coledge, he died. So brokenhearted and exhausted, she, too, became an easy victim of yellow fever.

"Her only wish was that she could be buried next to her lover.

"Special permission was granted by Congress and their graves are located side by side in Section 10. His remains are buried in Grave 1697 and hers in Grave 1698."

Either version, it's a heck of a story. ❧

New Ipswich

THIS LITTLE TOWN was, for many years, one of the most important places in New England. It was a center for banking and furniture-making. It had one of the first schools and the very first cotton mill in New Hampshire.

This area was first granted to Colonel John Wainwright and John Choat in 1735. The first settlers came here from Ipswich, Mass. And when the town was incorporated in 1762, they named it "Ipswich."

Four years later, because two towns named Ipswich posed some confusion, the townspeople petitioned to add the word "New" to their name. From that time on this has been New Ipswich.

Ipswich, by the way, is a city in England named after the Saxon Queen and Saint "Ebba" who lived about 530 A.D. and was the prioress at Coldingham Priory. "Wich" is the Saxon word for village and "Ebba's Wich," over the years, became "Eb's Wich" and then "Ipswich."

So there you have it.

The New Ipswich Academy dates to the late 1700s and was renowned all over New England. It was one of the first schools to acquire a pair of geographic globes, and its library boasted over a hundred books.

The weaving industrialist Samuel Appleton was born in New Ipswich, and he endowed the academy and was rewarded with its renaming as Appleton Academy. When I was growing up, this was the high school for New Ipswich. There were many schools that were originally private which towns took over for public education. Pinkerton Academy and Atkinson Academy are among the last of these schools with the original names.

Samuel Appleton's brother, Jesse, went on to become the president of Bowdoin College, and his daughter, Jane, married New Hampshire's only U.S. president, Franklin Pierce.

When the Mascenic Regional School was built, Appleton Academy became a private school again.

In the Highbridge section of town is the first cotton mill ever built in New Hampshire. It dates from 1804.

The Bank village section of New Ipswich is called so because, in Colonial times, it was a banking center.

And one of the great examples of Colonial architecture in New England is this: The Barrett Mansion, which is owned by the Society for the Preservation of New England Antiquities, and is open for tours to the public in the summertime.

The Hollywood motion picture *The Europeans*, based on the Henry James novel, was filmed at the Barrett Mansion a couple dozen years ago.

And beside the mansion is a graveyard with a curious stone. I have been unable to find the story of this stone other than what is here. It reads:

Mr. Gilman Spaulding
Was killed with an ax
By an insane Brother
Sept. 19,1842 Age 38 ❧

Plaistow

EVERYONE WHO FIRST runs across the name Plaistow mispronounces it. It angers many people in Plaistow to hear the pronunciation of their hometown butchered.

Makes you wonder where the spelling came from. Well, I think I know.

First of all, when the town was originally chartered back in 1749, Governor Benning Wentworth gave the town the name Plastow— P-L-A-S-T-O-W.

Yeah, you got it right, the first spelling of the town name did not contain an 'i.' That came later.

The area where Plaistow is now had been called a great many different names over the years. "Timburlain" for one, which is where the Timberlane school district gets its name.

But the area around what now is the town was also called, at one time, Policy Pond, Spricket Meadow and Amesbury Park.

Originally, all this was in Massachusetts and a part of Haverhill. Then, in 1746, the boundary was moved and Haverhill found its North Parish—its North Parish Meeting House—in another town; in fact, in another state.

The name Plastow was chosen, according to historian Elmer Munson Hunt, because it resembled an English Plaistowe which, according to him, is "an open space or greenwood near the center of the village where the maypole stood and where sports at holiday times were carried on."

Well . . . maybe. I have searched the Oxford dictionary and cannot find the word Plaistowe in any spelling. Now I'm not saying they are wrong,

But . . . here's what I think.

I think, right from the start, they called the place after the English town of Plaistow. Plaistow is near London, by the way.

Further, I think there was a misspelling of the original town name on the town charter and 50 years or so later some la-dee-dah person said, "It's named after the English town, and it should be spelled the same." And it was then they added the 'i' . . . and caused all these spelling and pronunciation problems.

But you know what else I think? I think the town should go back to the original spelling on the original charter, P-L-A-S-T-O-W.

That way, network news would not continually call the place "place-tow." Or . . . if the citizens here insist on keeping the present spelling (and, no doubt, they will, 'cause think of all the letterheads and e-mail addresses and signs and stuff that would have to be changed) . . . if they keep the spelling like the original English town, then they should pronounce it as the English do. In Plaistow, England, I'm told they pronounce it "plars-toe."

Now that's even fancier. Think of it . . . Timberlane school in Plarstoe. . . . ◆

The poem

IN DERRY, ON Pond Road near Beaver Pond, is a spot which was the inspiration for, perhaps, the most beloved American poem ever written.

For it was here, back in 1901, a man in a carriage paused to reflect on the fleetingness of life and of how painfully lovely some moments are. It was here that the poet first thought of the words familiar to every American schoolchild:

> *Whose woods these are I think I know*
> *His house is in the village though.*

Yes, the poet was Robert Frost, and in Derry is the spot where he actually stopped by the woods on a snowy evening. ❧

THE PEOPLE

Bezeleed Beckwith

IN ACWORTH, THE cemetery is located just down the hill from the center of town—out on a dirt road. It is a venerable place.

But the most interesting stone in the cemetery marks the grave of no one. It is the marker of Bezeleed Beckwith.

Beckwith died back when the Dartmouth Medical School and other places where doctors were trained needed cadavers for dissection, and about the only supply they could get was through the prisons. And the prisons could not supply enough.

Back then, there was commerce in fresh corpses, no questions asked. And poor Mr. Beckwith was buried and a day later dug up in the middle of the night and taken away.

His friends were so appalled that they placed a marker where he was once buried but was no more.

I swear, if there is a haunted cemetery anywhere, it is in Acworth. Even the trees are so healthy that they are stealing the stones, for their roots are fed with our ancestors. ❧

Colonel Benjamin Bellows

COLONEL BENJAMIN BELLOWS was the founder of the town of Walpole and the person for whom the town of Bellows Falls, Vermont, is named. Colonel Bellows came to Walpole when it was wilderness and lived to see it a prosperous community.

At the 250th celebration of the founding of Walpole, I read a description of the Bellows household that I found in a town history. Colonel Bellows lived in a style of large hospitality.

All strangers, travelers, and public men stopped at his house; and such was the number of hands his immense landed estate compelled him to employ, that his household had a matriarchal character.

A very large kitchen under the house, where a great oaken table lay always spread, was the eating-room of his workmen.

He always maintained a separate table for his immediate family saying, that next to religion itself, he held family ties sacred, and did not wish to have the sanctity of the fireside and the domestic board invaded by outsiders. The colonel raided his own stores and killed an ox or a cow every week to supply the wants of his household.

The winter stores were enormous in quantity, and the annual consumption fearful to contemplate. The colonel put down 20 barrels of port yearly; eggs were brought in by the half-bushel; and his men stipulated that they should not have salmon oftener than three times a week.

He made 400 barrels of cider per annum.

He had married his second wife, at Lunenburg, in April 1758, the widow of Jenison, whose maiden name was Mary Hubbard.

Their children were Abigail (after his daughter, I think, and not his first wife), Theodore, Thomas, Mary, and Josiah, all born between 1759 and 1767, so that at the time of his death he had nine children living, the youngest being 10 years old. ☙

Ruth Blay

IT HAPPENED IN New Hampton, back before the American Revolution. They brought Ruth Blay that winter day, dressed as a bride, to stand before the crowd.

Ruth Blay was 25 years old when she gave birth to a stillborn son in a room in a house in New Hampton. She had been a schoolteacher, and she was not married.

And so, in August of 1768, Ruth Blay had a baby . . . and buried the dead child. And told no one.

No one witnessed the birth. So who was to say the child was not born alive? Who was to say it was not murder?

The law in North Hampton in 1768 was English law. And English law was definite on the subject: To conceal the birth and death of an illegitimate child, murder or not, was punishable by hanging.

And so Ruth Blay was arrested. In November, she was brought before a justice. The law allowed for no exceptions. Ruth Blay was condemned to hang. Attorney General Clagett intoned to heaven that he was merely "discharging a duty that he owed his country, his King and his God."

The hanging was set for noon on December 31 in Portsmouth. Ruth Blay was not to see the New Year.

As the date approached, people debated the sentence. Most thought it unfair but it was the law. Many pleaded with Governor John Wentworth to intervene, to pardon the young woman. It was her only hope.

The dead infant was exhumed and examined by physicians. It was declared to be a stillbirth. It was not murder. Surely, the governor would now save her.

They built a gallows on the brow of the hill so that people could see the event. December 31 was cold. A thousand people gathered here.

Early that morning, a contingent had visited Governor Wentworth to beg for a formal reprieve. Word in the crowd was that the governor had signed such a paper and it was on the way; that there would be no hanging.

Then, from a distance, a terrible shrieking was heard. Soon a cart and horse appeared with the poor young woman begging the crowd, as she passed, to save her. She was dressed in silk, like a bride.

The cart was drawn under the gallows. The High Sheriff Thomas Packer mounted the cart and dropped the black cloth over the screaming girl's face and slipped the noose round her neck.

"Wait, wait," the crowd cried. "A pardon is on the way!"

But the town clock was already tolling noon.

High Sheriff Thomas Packer stepped down from the cart. "I will not be late for my dinner," he said. "Draw the cart away!"

And, dressed as a bride, Ruth Blay went to meet her maker.

Five minutes later, the pardon arrived from the governor.

The crowd, by the way, rioted. That night the sheriff was hanged in effigy in front of his home and on the hanging figure was pinned a paper with this written on it:

> *Am I to lose my dinner*
> *This woman for to hang?*
> *Draw away the cart my boys*
> *Don't stop to say amen.*

The sheriff was a wealthy man when he died in his sleep of old age.

Ruth Blay was buried just a few feet away from where she was hanged . . . in an unmarked grave in Portsmouth. ❧

Willa Cather

IN THE SOUTHWESTERN corner of the Jaffrey Center Cemetery, under the pine trees in the shadow of Monadnock Mountain, lie the remains of, perhaps, the greatest writer and poet of the American Great Plains.

Here is the grave of Willa Cather.

The woman who loved the prairies more than life itself is interred, not beneath great expanses of Kansas, but amidst the colonial founders of this historical New England village.

The question, of course, is why. And, yes, there is a story.

In the early 1940s Willa Cather and her companion were on summer vacation when they discovered Shattuck Inn in Jaffrey. Willa Cather knew the Monadnock region because of her relationship with the MacDowell Colony in Peterborough. MacDowell, in case you don't know, is the oldest artist colony in America.

At the Shattuck Inn, Willa Cather found a place to write away from the heat of the city and the incursions of the world. And one evening when the light was perfect over Monadnock, she and her friend sat on the veranda, and Miss Cather noted that it would be nice to spend eternity here.

Willa Cather died in April 1947 and, true to her request, her friend had her interred in the old Jaffrey Center Cemetery. And years later when she died also, she came here to lie for eternity beside her friend. ☙

The Chases

IT WAS THE biggest event in the history of Washington, New Hampshire: a funeral, a funeral with a procession that was a hundred cars long.

It was October 19, 1933. People had come from all the great cities in the Northeast. The cortège wound for miles and ended here. And here, in Washington, hundreds of people stood and sang, not "Nearer My God to Thee" but rather, "The International."

For these people were mostly communists and they had come to pay their respects to a man they considered a hero and a comrade. The comrade was Fred Chase.

Shocking, isn't it? A large granite monument with a hammer and sickle, here in Washington amidst the Christian crosses.

Also engraved on the stone is the name of Fred Chase's wife, Elba; and to the sides the graves of some of their children. Communists all.

So, what's the story here?

Well, it's a story of a man and his wife and their five children; a family growing up before and during the great American Depression.

Fred Chase came from Keene. The family has been here for hundreds of years. Salmon P. Chase, Lincoln's secretary of war, was a relative. Elba's family, the Korbs, came from Latvia. They arrived here when she was 13.

Both Fred and Elba were unionists. They were also activists. Fred's interest was in farmers. Elba was a millworker and later a nurse in Boston. They were married and started a family. In 1915, the family moved to a farm a couple miles down the hill from the center of town. The Chases continued to attend Socialist Party conventions around the country. In 1928, Fred became the president of the New Hampshire chapter of the Worker's Party. This was later to become the Communist Party.

In 1930, Fred put his name on the New Hampshire ballot as the Communist Party candidate for governor. In 1932, he ran for the U.S. Senate. He lost both elections by a landslide. He only received three votes in his hometown.

Hard farm work and the strain of running for office took its toll and, in 1933, Fred suffered a massive heart attack from which he did not recover. He died within a month. He was 52.

But the family activism did not die with Fred. In 1938, Elba ran for governor as the communist candidate. She, too, of course, lost by a landslide. Elba died in 1964.

Their youngest son, Oliver, continued the struggle until his death in 1984. He, too, had a large funeral but those who attended were neighbors and friends.

And how did the citizens of New Hampshire and the town of Washington feel about the Chases? Well, they were regularly denounced in the *Union Leader* and during the McCarthy era. The state attorney general, Louis Wyman, tried to bring charges against Elba but nothing came of it. She was, however, regularly pilloried in the New Hampshire House and Senate.

But in Washington people knew the Chases as good friends. They minded their own business. They helped their neighbors. Elba, especially, was known to use her skill as a nurse when her fellow townspeople were ill. Both the Chases were members of the town library committee.

They lived a hard and modest life on their farm. Fellow communists would come from other parts of the country to spend some time with the Chases, but they were often poor farmers like themselves. The attorney general regarded them as evil incarnate but no one in Washington saw them as a threat. They were, frankly, as were their children, well liked.

And since the fall of the Berlin Wall everything has changed. This brutal communist symbol is now sort of a misnomer. Kruschev said, "We will bury you." But the opposite has happened; we have buried them. And not with soil, but like the monument in Washington, New Hampshire, with flowers. ◆

Goodie Cole

THE WOMAN ACCUSED was Goodwife Eunice Cole. They called her "Goodie."

It was 1670. Goodie Cole was 64 years old. Her husband William was 10 years older than she. The couple owned some valuable salt marsh property in town.

Goodie was outspoken and eccentric. She had a mouth on her. She attracted attention. She may have been schizophrenic. When some cows in Hampton turned up missing, neighbors claimed that the cows had eaten grass from Goodie's field and had thus been cursed.

Some neighborhood kids said they had seen Goodie take the form of a cat. They also said they had seen a black dwarf with a red cap eating at her table. It was Satan himself, they said.

Finally a local boat on the way to Boston sank off Boar's Head at Hampton. Everyone was lost. Goodie, it was said, had cursed the ship.

Two hundred years later the poet John Greenleaf Whittier wrote a poem about the cursed ship entitled, "The Wreck of Rivermouth." Whittier wrote the poem while a guest at Celia Thaxter's hotel out on Appledore Island on the Isles of Shoals.

Some of the poem reads:

> Oh Rivermouth rocks, how sad a sight
> Ye saw in the light of breaking day!
> Dead faces looking up cold and white
> From sand and seaweed where they lay.
> The mad old witch-wife wailed and wept,
> And cursed the tide as it backward crept;
> "Crawl back; crawl back; blue water snake!
> Leave your dead for the hearts that break."

Goodie Cole was brought before the court and charged with witchcraft. She was sentenced to 40 lashes with a whip and "life in prison."

Her husband William was required to pay the court expenses. He claimed that he relied on his wife for keeping the finances. For his petition, the court confiscated his land and sold it at auction.

Goodie petitioned the commonwealth for release and, after 15 years, she was allowed to go home to Hampton. She was 81 years old. It wasn't until she arrived home that she learned that her husband had died.

The court billed Hampton for the costs of her care over the 15 years she was incarcerated. When the town failed to meet a payment, one of the selectmen was jailed until the money was coughed up.

In the meantime, Goodie lived in a hovel on the hill. Townspeople were required to bring her food.

It is no wonder that the old accusations cropped up again. She was charged once more with having "familiarity with the devil," found guilty and sentenced again to prison where she remained for only a few months this time. She was sent again to be a ward of the town.

People again brought food to her doorstep, but one day the food was not taken in. Neighbors broke into the shanty and found Goodie dead in her bed. She was 88.

Legend has it that a mob took Goodie's body to a field where they drove a wooden stake though her heart. It is not known where she was buried, certainly not in a Christian graveyard. ◄

Betty Davis story

I ONCE PEED on Bette Davis. Yes, it's true.

My Aunt Mimi had been a student, along with Bette, at an academy down in Ashburnham, Mass., back in the early '20s. Bette and Mimi remained friends until Mimi died in 1946.

Anyhoo, when I was just a couple months old, Bette visited Mimi and my mother at Mimi's home on Oak Street in Manchester. She was passing through on her way north and stopped for a visit. I was there and Bette asked to hold me, and I was apparently impressed. And she said, "Maybe you better take him back." Some might say this incident set a pattern for my entire life.

Bette Davis and New Hampshire go way back.

She was born close by, in Lowell, Mass. Back in 1908. Her mother, Ruthie, divorced her dad right after Bette was born. In 1926, when Bette was 18, her mom moved her and her sister to Peterborough. Yes, Peterborough. They lived in an apartment up on Vine Street, in a building that is still there.

That summer Bette took dance and acting classes at the Mari Arden outdoor summer theater, out on old Hancock road. The Mari Arden was one of the first summer theaters in America.

Her mother, Ruth, supported her family as a professional photographer. She took all the yearbook photographs of the Peterborough High School Class of '27.

Bette married her first husband when she was 28. Ham Nelson was his name. Bette's second husband was one Arthur Farnsworth. She married him in 1940. Farnsworth was unlike Bette's other husbands in that he had no connection to show business. He was a socialite and an intellectual . . . a very bright and charming man, and he adored Bette. They were, by all accounts, madly in love.

They had summered at the hotels in Sugar Hill up in the White Mountains. They regarded the town as their special place. Soon they set about making a lovely summer home out of an old barn located on a hillside outside of town. They called the home, "Butternut." It still exists.

Of course, the entire state of New Hampshire was agog. Jeez, Bette Davis living in a little town in the White Mountains.

On April fourth, 1941, Bette celebrated her 33rd birthday in a way that is still talked of north of the notches.

That weekend the Eponymous Premiere Theater in Littleton was selected to hold a world premiere of one of Bette's films, "The Great Lie."

Ten thousand people crowded downtown Littleton to cheer the diva and wish her "Happy Birthday."

Aside from the movie premiere, there were parties and parades and a gala birthday ball at the opera house complete with the largest birthday cake ever baked in the history of the state—200 pounds . . . five feet high . . . 30 feet around. All the national press covered the event as well as a live radio broadcast that went all over New England. To this day, the celebration remains the greatest party ever held in the history of Littleton.

Bette Davis and Arthur Farnsworth stayed at Butternut Farm until his death of a heart attack two years later. He was buried there at the farm. Bette could see the grave from their bedroom window.

Two years later, Bette remarried, to William Grant Sherry. Bette and her new husband summered at "Butternut" and one day, without any fanfare, Arthur Farnsworth's grave was gone. He was removed to Vermont. A year later the farm was sold. Five years later, Bette divorced Sherry and married for the last time.

Her new husband was actor Gary Merrill. They lived in Maine until that marriage ended in 1960.

Bette died in France in 1989. She is buried in Forest Lawn Cemetery in Hollywood.

The world loved her, but no place loved her more than New Hampshire did.

And I . . . I am truly sorry I peed on her. ✐

Hannah Davis

HER DAD, PETER Davis, was a clockmaker who plied business in Jaffrey at the start of the 19th Century. She learned much about wood and veneers from him.

But Peter Davis died and left his widow and teen-age daughter to fend for themselves.

The young woman did what she had to do. She had skills in woodworking that she got from her dad. But more importantly, she had a sense of what would sell, and she set about creating a product that became a sensation and made her a wealthy woman.

The product was the bandbox. And the woman was Hannah Davis. She is buried here in the Jaffrey Center Cemetery.

The band boxes ranged in size from small, hand-bag size containers to boxes that would hold as much as a large suitcase would today.

When she had a number of boxes ready, Hannah herself would drive a Conestoga wagon from Jaffrey down to the mills in Lowell or Manchester or Lawrence. She would park outside the factory gates and the young women would swarm around and purchase her boxes. Here was a way to carry fashions bought in the city back home for visits. Here was an elegant way to store clothing.

The boxes sold for from 12 to 50 cents depending on their size. This may seem cheap but 50 cents represented a full day's work to many of these women.

Nowadays Hannah Davis bandboxes are in museums all over the world and many have retained their structure and beauty for 150 years.

The *Jaffrey Town History* tells us that Hannah Davis lived a life of kindness and goodwill and became the most-beloved person in the region. Everyone knew her as "Aunt" Hannah Davis. Aunt Hannah died November 29, 1863. She was 79. ❧

Ruel Durkee

GEORGE GEERS PHOTOGRAPH

The statue of Franklin Pierce looks upon the Eagle Hotel.

THE BUILDING RIGHT across from the New Hampshire Statehouse is the Eagle Hotel. Nowadays it is senior housing, but there was a time when the great personages of the world were guests here. And, of course, a lot of political dealing went on here.

From before the time of the Civil War and up into the 1880s, a man named Ruel Durkee controlled the state government from chambers on the north side of the first floor. He held court in what was affectionately called the "throne room."

Durkee was from Croydon, a little town just north of Newport, and he came by his power by lending money to legislators and, sometimes, he was repaid with favors.

As years passed he became the liaison between the railroad interests and the legislature. This was as much power as could be had in the 1800s.

Here is a place where Andrew Jackson slept and Jefferson Davis, Benjamin Harrison, even Eleanor Roosevelt, and Charles Lindberg stayed here.

There had been a hotel in this place earlier. It burned to the ground in 1851 only to be rebuilt the next year just in time to celebrate the inauguration of New Hampshire's own president, Franklin Pierce.

By 1870, a person could go from downtown Concord to downtown Boston on the train in less time than it takes to drive that distance today. Railroads meant power. A town without the railroad was relegated to the past. A town with a railroad would prosper.

Durkee decided which towns and which railroads went where in the state. And he held his power by providing free passes to those in the legislature who voted his way.

For close to 50 years no man became governor or senator or congressman without the blessing of Ruel Durkee.

And, by the way, this was the time of Sen. John Chandler, of editor and author Sarah Josepha Hale, of President Ulysses Grant. And you will find this entire cast of characters in this book, *Coniston,* by Winston Churchill.

That is not, by the way, the Winston Churchill of World War II fame. This Winston Churchill lived here in New Hampshire, over in Cornish. In his time, he was the number-one selling author in the entire country and his number-one best seller was this book.

It's a "roman a clef," that is, the names have been changed. But, unlike most novels that say "any resemblance to anyone is coincidental," this book says "everyone herein is based on an actual person." And the Newport Library has a key that identifies all the characters.

Also this book is trash. It's such an easy read! It's a comedy, a history, and a very sexy love story written with lots of short sentences and active verbs. In other words, "a page-turner."

Your library has a copy, I'm sure.

Coniston, by Winston Churchill. What fun! ❧

Hannah Dustin

A statue of Hannah Dustin stands on the island in Penacook
where the Contoocook and Merrimack rivers join.

HAVERHILL IS THE very spot where it happened . . . a terrible, bloody tragedy . . . This was the spring of 1697. A long time ago.

They named the baby, Martha. She was their 12th child, of whom eight survived. But Martha's birth had been a difficult one and her mother, Hannah, had taken to her bed. The baby was fussy. Mary Neff, a woman from next door, had come to live with the family, to nurse the child and care for the mother.

The family lived, by the way, on what was then the frontier, close by the Merrimack River in what is now Haverhill, Mass.

Thomas was a farmer. He was also a constable for the community. The community was then comprised of less than a hundred people.

Now, this was during the French and Indian Wars, and there had been Indian attacks all over Massachusetts. Thomas and Hannah were on their guard. It was the ides of March, on March 15, it happened.

Early that afternoon, Thomas and his children were in the field clearing rocks when they looked up to see party of about 20 Abenaki Indians in full war paint and dress. There were still patches of snow on the ground. Thomas herded the kids together and mounted his horse, and they all scrambled for the cabin yelling all the time for Hannah and Mary to get ready to flee. The women heard them coming and looked out to see the children running in front and Thomas keeping a rear guard.

They reached the cabin, with Thomas yelling for them to get ready to mount the horse. They must get to the garrison house. There they could defend themselves. But Hannah was barefoot in her nightgown, and the baby was fussing and there was no time.

Thomas and the children approached outside the cabin but the Indians were closing in. Hannah hollered that he must save the children and leave at once. She would fend for herself. Mary, the nurse, also refused to go. She was needed for the child.

And so, Thomas and the children made their way to safety, and the Indians came and kicked in the cabin door. They entered the room and began ransacking. They took pots and utensils and all tools they found. They pulled the women outside. But the baby, Martha, was screaming. One Indian took the child by the ankles and swung her at the door jamb . . . bashing her skull in and killing her instantly.

All over Haverhill similar atrocities were happening. By day's end forty people would be dead or captured.

The women were forced to the river's edge and into a canoe. Hannah looked back to see her home in flames. She was barefoot.

The party then set off up the Merrimack. They would first be taken to an Indian village where, they were told, they would be stripped and made to run the gauntlet. If they lived, from there they would be marched to Canada where they would be ransomed by the French.

The river was swollen by melting snow and spring rains. There was a fierce current which they paddled against. At times the women were forced to walk. For two entire weeks they traveled up river. They finally landed here, on this island, located at the confluence of the Merrimack and Contoocook rivers.

Here Hannah and Mary were given over to a much smaller contingent of Native Americans. They would await another party of Indians and then be taken to their village.

The Native Americans on the island consisted of two older men, three women and seven children.

Here they met a third captive. This was a 13-year-old English lad named Samuel Leonardson. Sam had immigrated to what is now Worcester and had been captured by the Abenaki there more than a year before.

In the year he lived with the Native Americans, he had learned their language and many of their ways. But he was always looking for an escape, and this opportunity looked good to him.

That night Sam, Hannah and Mary plotted what they would do. Early the next morning, before sunrise, the trio awoke and gathered the weapons from the sleeping Indians.

Sam had learned from the tribe where to hit a person with a tomahawk in order to kill him. He instructed Hannah and Mary, and the three went to work. They killed both men and one woman in their sleep. The other two women now awoke, and they were on one of them at once. The second woman escaped, running to a canoe.

They then killed six of the seven children. They had become fond of one of the boys and could not bring themselves to kill him. Of course, he was frightened and ran off as soon as he got the chance.

Samuel Leonard had also learned how to scalp. He showed the women how. They took scalps from all 10 corpses. They then smashed in all but one canoe and, taking what food there was, started down river.

This time the current was with them and they reached what is now Nashua in a single day.

All were paid a bounty of 50 pounds for the scalps they had and were showered with presents from the governor and other well-wishers.

The story itself was written down by Cotton Mather in his *Magnanlia Christi Americana* and has become a legend learned by schoolchildren all over New England.

There is a statue of Hannah in the center of Haverhill and another on the island where it all happened.

The woman was, of course, Hannah Dustin. ◈

Thorvald Eriksson

NORSE HISTORY TELLS us that in 1004, 250 Vikings sailed in four ships from Iceland to Newfoundland to establish a permanent settlement.

Norse history also tells us the settlement was a failure. One ship was blown off course and the crew ended as slaves in Ireland.

Those who got to America fought amongst themselves and slaughtered Native Americans left and right.

The Vikings also may have explored as far south as Cape Cod.

One of the captains of the ships exploring the coast was Leif Eriksson's brother Thorvald. Thorvald and his crew killed Native Americans whenever they found them.

In the summer of 1006, they came ashore somewhere on the northeast coast and found a camp of nine sleeping Indians. The Vikings stabbed eight of them to death as they lay. One escaped. The next morning, the Native Americans found Thorvald's ship and attacked it. Thorvald took an arrow in the armpit and died.

A lot of people over the years have thought that Thorvald Eriksson was killed on the shore in Hampton. Why? Because of a gravestone.

A stone is, in fact, on display outside the Tuck Museum in Hampton. The stone was found some years ago on land belonging to the Lamprey Family. The carved lines on the stone resemble Viking runes.

Is it Thorvald Eriksson's gravestone?

The simple answer is, "no." There are no Norse runes that look like this carving and a lot of scholars feel that they may have been carved, not in the year 1006 but rather in 1926 or sometime there about.

Also they know Thorvald died up near the St. Lawrence River, not down here near the Hampton Casino.

But a lot of Viking sagas are also myths. Why not this one? ✎

Viggo Brandt Erickson

IN THE NORTHWEST corner of the Jaffrey Center cemetery is the face of a young woman, Dorothy Caldwell Erickson.

Dorothy was in Paris back before the First World War when she met and married a dashing young Scandinavian sculptor, Viggo Brandt Erickson. Soon the couple was expecting a child. But all was not well and the mother and daughter both died in childbirth. The bodies were cremated, the child in his mother's arms.

In his grief, Viggo brought their ashes back to his wife's home and he created this tomb.

Viggo stayed in Jaffrey the rest of his life and is, in fact, the creator of the "Buddies" statue on the Jaffrey Common.

He remarried and, when his second wife passed away, he again produced a unique monument to her memory, a gentle pastel creation in the Conant Cemetery.

And, yes, the two women are buried in separate cemeteries. ✎

Amos Fortune

IN THE JAFFREY Center Cemetery you may read an entire family history engraved on the slate of two gravestones.

These are the graves of Amos Fortune and his wife Violet.

Amos Fortune was a black slave captured on the Guinea Coast sometime around 1725. He was sold to a Boston tanner who taught him to read and write. By the age of 52, he had managed to save enough money to purchase his freedom from his owner.

He then came north to Jaffrey and set up a tannery here. It thrived, and Amos Fortune built a home that still exists. With the money he made, he purchased a wife and gave her freedom.

He died in November of 1801 at the age of 91 and left much of his estate to the Congregational Church and to the Jaffrey schools. The Amos Fortune Forums are a lecture series held every Friday evening at the Center Meeting House.

His wife died just a year after him.

Their stones tell their story better than any other testament.

His reads:

Sacred to the memory of Amos Fortune who was born free in Africa, a slave in America, he purchased liberty, professed Christianity, lived reputably, and died hopefully. November 17, 1801, age 91

And Violet's stone reads

Sacred to the memory of Violet, by sale the slave of Amos Fortune, by marriage his wife, by her fidelity his friend and solace. She died his widow September 13, 1802. Age 73

Horace Greeley

This stone honoring Horace Greeley sits in the Amherst Town Common.

THE OTHER DAY I was looking through this scrapbook my grandfather put together back in 1883.

It is full of lots of stuff he found interesting—poems and obituaries, articles about people he knew. Most of the stuff in the scrapbook comes from the *Milford Cabinet* . . . including a really juicy article discussing Horace Greeley.

No doubt you know that Horace Greeley was born in New Hampshire, here in Amherst. The house he was born in still exists. Today it is a beautiful home, all the more appealing for its history.

When I was a kid the place looked more like the hardscrabble farm it was back in 1811 when Horace was born there. Hardscrabble is the right phrase. And I don't mean a difficult word game. I mean a place full of rocks and not-so-good soil. It was cold and damp and depressing. Not the place you might think the most powerful man in America got his early education. And, yes, Horace Greeley became the most powerful man in the country. He was the publisher of the most popular and most radical newspaper in the northern states . . . The New York Tribune.

Horace lived his first 14 years on this farm. He was an odd-looking kid, pasty white and kinda soft . . . who kids today would call "a brain." He was smart and precocious . . . learned to read by the time he was three. Read the local newspaper from front to back every week. The newspaper was the *Cabinet*. Today it is the *Milford Cabinet*. Then it was published in Horace's hometown, Amherst.

OK. Let's get to the juicy stuff.

The article is in grandmother's scrapbook. The piece is by Grace M. Roach, whose family published the *Cabinet* until this year. Talk about history!

Anyhow, the story tells of how Horace proposed marriage to one Mary Cheeney, a schoolteacher from Connecticut. Here's the story as told to Grace Roach by a person who knew Greeley personally, one Mrs. R. E. White.

His interest in the lady was awakened when a friend who told him the story of Miss Cheeney and brought about a correspondence between them.

The interests on both sides grew and deepened until Mr. Greeley, in his straightforward way of asking for whatever he wanted, asked her to be his wife, and she, knowing only his mental qualities, and in fancy, clothing him with personal graces suited to so fine a character, let her imagination take her captive . . . and accepted him.

It was arranged that Mr. Greeley should go south, spend one day, be married, and return north immediately. The hour of meeting was one which both parties anticipated with strange feelings of curiosity. They met and stood face to face. Miss Cheeney, in her youth and beauty, was quite as charming as Mr. Greeley's ideal of her. But she was breathless with shocked amazement at his appearance.

His flaxen-white hair was long and fell around his neck loosely; his face was as fair as a woman's, and its expression noble; he had a dimpled chin and a mouth of manly firmness, an index to his character that redeemed the face from effeminacy. But the figure was painfully without grace, his voice extremely drawling and nasal, and in his manner was a total disregard for accepted rules of etiquette.

Miss C. could not conceal her disappointment.

But they sat down to arrange the business part of an immediate marriage.

Mr. G., in his delight, failed to see her dismay. "Can you go now?" he asked.

"Go where?"

"Go to be married," was the reply.

"To be married! Why I cannot marry you. Now that I see you. I do not love you," she said, half-choked by tears.

His surprise was greater than hers. Then came to his aid that firm strong will. He stifled pride and insisted Miss. C. should keep her engagement with him.

She afterward said that she felt under a spell and that he had a strange influence over her that rendered her submissive. She looked at his travel-stained clothes and boots and asked him to prepare for the marriage, but to understand that she had no love for him.

Mr. G. went at all speed to a barber and, in a proud air, told the man he was to be married in less than an hour.

"Brush off my clothes," he ordered.

The barber, with brush in hand suspended in air, asked, "Not going to change this suit?"

"No, no, brought no other. Go on, brush off the dirt."

"But sir, look at the bottom of your trousers; the stains will show."

"Never mind. Cut off the bottom."

And that was it.

They went to a minister with his pants cut off like clam diggers and they were married and, from all accounts, lived happily in New York for the rest of their lives. They had seven kids, five of whom died. Only two daughters survived them.

In 1872, Greeley ran for president against Ulysses Grant. Toward the end of the campaign, his beloved Mary died. Greeley was inconsolable. On top of his grief, Grant trounced him in the election. A month later, his heart broken, Horace Greeley died.

It was noted in the newspapers that more people attended his funeral than had attended Lincoln's funeral. It was a hell of a life. And it all started here in Milford. ❧

Captain John Gunnison

GOSHEN HAS LESS than a thousand people. It is, and always has been, a small town—a general store, town hall, library, building supplies, all lined up on Route 10, about 10 miles south of Newport.

But in front of the Olive G. Pettis Library is a state historical marker informing us that Captain John W. Gunnison was born here in 1812.

And who was Captain John W. Gunnison?

Well, the marker tells us that he was a schoolteacher in Goshen, then went to West Point. After graduation, he became an Army officer and a surveyor. He mapped the Great Lakes and much of Utah. The marker also informs us that he wrote the first history of the Mormons and the Mormon Church and that, in 1853, while leading a survey for the Pacific Railroad, his expedition was attacked by Indians, and he was killed by bow and arrow.

Well, I have looked into this, and I have found out there is a lot more to this story.

Seems there is a question of whether it was simply Indians who killed Captain Gunnison.

Out on the Internet, I found a letter written to Captain Gunnison's wife by the judge who tried the Indians accused of his murder. Twenty-six were charged, but only eight were brought to trial. Of those, only two were young men. The rest were old men and women and children. They were dismissed out of hand. The two remaining got only a couple years in prison. The prosecution was such a travesty that the judge on the case, Judge William W. Drummond, resigned his position as a justice in the Utah Territory.

In November of 1853, Captain Gunnison and a half dozen of his men were encamped by the Servier River in Utah Territory. The attack came from across the river. The men were shot as they stood.

Then, according to the judge, with a great whoop, men of the Parvante tribe forded the stream and dispatched the wounded, including Captain Gunnison. It was a bloody business. All were scalped, some alive. The wounded had their arms and legs severed as they died.

Captain Gunnison's heart was cut out of his body as he lay wounded and, according to testimony, cut into pieces and laid on his chest.

An Indian warrior named Eneis, in another trial, claimed that Captain Gunnison's party was brought down by members of a Mormon group, and the Indians had only done their savagery afterwards. It was, he testified, all political and was planned beforehand by members of the faith. He testified further that the tribesmen had been given instruction not to scalp or mutilate the two members of the church who were in the party . . . that is, Gunnison and one other, and that they could be identified by their robes which they wore next to their bodies under their other garments.

But the instruction was ignored and all were massacred.

The letter to Mrs. Gunnison does not say why the attack was done but, at the time, the Mormon Church had very bad relations with the U.S. government, and a surveying team was not welcome. Also, Gunnison's history of the church was an honest history as he saw and wrote it, and it was resented.

But, I must say, none of this was ever proved and, to this day, as it states on the historic marker in Goshen, the official story is that Captain Gunnison and his men were ambushed and killed solely by Indians. ◆

Hutchinson Family Singers

MY GRANDMOTHER KNEW John Hutchinson. She liked him.

John was the final remaining member of the famous Hutchinson Family Singers. He lived, as did all the Hutchinsons, in Milford.

The Hutchinson homestead still exists in Milford ... on the North River Road. It was here that Jesse Hutchinson and his wife Mary raised their family. There were 15 children of whom 11 lived to adulthood.

They are all buried here in a cemetery just down the way from the homestead. Oh, you may not know who the Hutchinson Family Singers were. Well, let me tell you:

The Hutchinson Family Singers were the most popular singing group in America from a time just before the Civil War until about the turn of the 20th century.

In their time, the Hutchinson Family Singers were as well known in this country as, say, Brittany Spears is now.

They traveled the world singing songs of emancipation and women's rights and of temperance. The Hutchinson Family Singers hated slavery and alcohol and they wanted the vote for women. They were zealous in their cause and would not soften their opinions for anyone. As a result, they were either greatly loved or despised. There was no middle ground with the Hutchinsons.

Abraham Lincoln heard them sing many times and loved them. But all over the South they were hated for their stand on slavery.

Frederick Douglass was a house guest at the homestead many times and so was P.T. Barnum. And, in fact, Tom Thumb came to Milford on his honeymoon and rode a miniature coach pulled by two ponies in the back door of the house and down the hall and out the front door to the great applause of those present.

Milford in the 1850s was a hotbed of abolitionist activity and the Hutchinson homestead was a major stop on the underground railroad that helped slaves escape to Canada.

Right at the start of the Civil War, however, there was an incident that made all the newspapers when the Hutchinson Singers sang for the Union soldiers just outside of Washington D.C. They sang songs of emancipation and were shocked when they were soundly booed by the troops. There was almost a riot over the matter and, thenceforth, the Hutchinsons were never again invited to sing for the Army.

They had thought that the fight was for the end of slavery but most of the troops, it seems, felt it was a fight for keeping the union. It wasn't until the "Emancipation Proclamation" was issued that slavery became a rallying cry for the war.

And, by the way, years after the Civil War, the Hutchinson Singers found themselves aboard a ferry ship one evening where none other than General Robert E. Lee himself was a guest. The family sang for the general, and Robert E. Lee sent a bottle of wine to their table. They thanked him although all were tea drinkers and epoused temperance.

The Hutchinsons sang for a generation and carried on the tradition until 1908 when the last of the tribe, John Hutchinson, passed away. He was the one my grandmother knew.

And, how did the Hutchinson Family Singers sound? Well, you have to realize that these were times before amplification. Singers had to fill entire auditoriums with the strength of their voices.

Also, the times were simpler and the audiences less sophisticated . . . Well, what I'm trying not to say, is that they were pretty bad. One Hutchinson song is called "The Tribe of Jesse"—Jesse being their dad. And in this song they give all their names . . . the lyric goes: "David, Noah, Andrew, Zeffie . . . Caleb, Joshua, Jess and Benjie . . . Judson, John and Asa . . . and Abby are our names." ❧

Marquis de Lafayette

IN 1825, THE Marquis de Lafayette made a tour of his adopted country, the United States of America. He was, at the time, 76 years old. He had come to see how the country he had fought and bled for was fairing.

In case you don't remember, Lafayette was wounded in the leg at Brandywine and served with George Washington at Valley Forge.

On his return to France, Lafayette was a hero to his countrymen but later, when the French had their own revolution, he and his wife and two daughters barely escaped the guillotine. They, however, spent two years in a prison dungeon. Later, he and his family were pardoned by Napoleon.

In 1824, President James Monroe invited Lafayette to visit the country that he loved and that so loved him. He accepted and, in August, arrived in New York City. Before he went back to France, he had visited all 24 states that were then in the Union. From New York, the Marquis traveled north to visit Boston and Charlestown, where he helped lay the cornerstone of the Bunker Hill Monument. He then came to Portsmouth. Then traveled south.

Nearly a year later, in June, Lafayette was back in New Hampshire on his way to Vermont and upper New York State. On his way to Concord, he stopped in Suncook village to visit with the son of his old military friend, General John Stark.

Major Caleb Stark had written Lafayette to invite him to come meet his wife and family. When Lafayette stepped from his coach, Major Stark bounded up and shook his hand. He then launched into a long and boring speech about Revolutionary times. He had, the *Pembroke Town History* tells us, utterly forgotten his family who were standing near awaiting an introduction. Finally, Stark's oldest daughter could stand it no longer and she stepped forth and grasped Lafayette's hand.

"Permit me to introduce myself to you as the eldest daughter of Major Caleb Stark with whom you are talking," she said. "I am also the granddaughter of General John Stark, the hero of Bennington.

And now," she said, "permit me to introduce you to my mother, brothers, and sisters."

And then she did just that, with her dad just kinda standing there.

As he was leaving, Lafayette noted to an aide that the young woman possessed all the fire and spirit that her grandfather had possessed. ❧

The jailer Toby Lakeman

THIS IS A story of trust and betrayal . . . and redemption and love. It is about a man who was the local police deputy and jail keeper. His name was Tobias Lakeman.

Mr. Lakeman lived with his family in a house attached to the old Portsmouth Jailhouse that used to be over on Middle Street. For a jailer, Toby Lakeman was a kind-hearted and trusting person.

Now back then—and "back then" was about 1735—the local jailer had a lot of discretion regarding prisoners.

For instance here: Seems that half a dozen Quakers were arrested for heresy and were ordered to trial. Toby knew these people and he, on his own accord, let them leave the jail and go home—simply on their promise to return of their own accord for the trial.

They did not disappoint him. They arrived for their trial as promised, and the jailer had saved the costs of their pre-trial incarceration.

All well and good, but another friend of his, a "gentleman" debtor, was arrested and also promised Toby that he would appear for trial. So Toby allowed him to go home also. Big mistake.

The bounder bounded, and left Toby to explain to the court why he was not there.

The judge, in his wisdom, charged poor Toby and his family for the amount the so-called gentleman owed. It was a great amount.

The Lakeman family lost its home, and Toby was fired from his job. They were paupers. The former jailer went mad, it is said, and alone roamed from town to town all his life. He was gentle and friendly, but quite batty. And he lived to a great old age.

Well into his 90s, this thin, gray, bent man with worn but clean clothing would visit families from New Ipswich to Newbury Port. He would arrive at their door and was always welcomed.

For his story was well known and, by the end of his life, had reached the point of being almost a myth. It was an honor to have him at your table.

For he was always good company and sweet-natured. And deeply loved. ✒

Hermit Ben Lear

IT IS ALMOST impossible to be a hermit nowadays.

But back a couple hundred years there were lots of hermits.

In the late 1700s, Portsmouth was a busy metropolis. But even in this urban place there was a hermit.

His name was Benjamin Lear and he lived in a shack down on the south side of Sagamore Creek. This is where Route 1 is nowadays; all urban sprawl. Back then though, it was farmland and wilderness. And right there was a shack and a barn and pastures.

The farm had been bigger when Benjamin Lear was a lad. It had belonged to his parents. But then his dad died, and Ben and his mom lived in the shack.

He farmed just as much as he needed and no more. And, aside from enough land to keep a cow or two, the place went to seed.

Ben and his mother survived mostly on potatoes and milk. And they kept to themselves.

The diet I guess was OK. Mrs. Lear lived to be over a hundred years old.

There is a story told by writer Charles Brewster about a neighbor visiting the Lear shanty. Mrs. Lear burst into tears when she heard a bell tolling for a funeral. She told the visitor she was so tired. "When will the bell toll for me?" she asked. "I am afraid that I shall never die!"

But she did die, and Ben was able to further consolidate his assets. He also made his clothes of his own design. It is said that he went to town only once or twice a year and he called the town, "The Bank," after its original name "Strawbery Banke."

Although Benjamin Lear eschewed company, he was not a curmudgeon. Rather, he was a smiling man of moderate temper. People liked him but knew he preferred solitude and so stayed away.

When he got old, his neighbors offered to house him in the winter so that he might be more comfortable. But Ben Lear stayed in his shanty. In his 80s, Brewster writes, "Owing no doubt to his simple and temperate mode of living, he exhibited a face freer from wrinkles than is generally seen in those of fifty."

The hermit Benjamin Lear died in his shanty on December 17, 1802. He was eighty two.

He became ill, but would allow no one into his home. The night before his death, the temperature fell to four degrees below zero. He died the next morning.

When they found him, he was clothed in old, tattered rags with a single blanket over him as he lay on a straw pallet. Alone to the end.

And today, as we go for a double cheeseburger with fries and a thick shake at McDonalds, few of us know that just down the hill there is a spot of land where, in another time, a man had lived his whole life never having tasted anything other than potatoes and milk. ❧

Major Andrew McClary

MAJOR ANDREW MCCLARY came from Epsom.

His name may be familiar to you as it was to me, but somehow unidentifiable.

Major McClary, it turns out, is the man for whom Fort McClary is named. McClary is one of those forts that guard Portsmouth Harbor.

Major McClary is famous for leading the New Hampshire Twelfth Militia Regiment at the Battle of Bunker Hill. The regiment was made up of men from Epsom, Deerfield, Northwood, Chichester, Pittsfield and Nottingham.

The battle at Lexington took place on, as Longfellow tells us, "the nineteenth of April in seventy-five."

Word of Lexington and Concord was received in New Hampshire, and the locals heard that we were to face the British in Boston. Hundreds of men rushed to the parade grounds in Nottingham. There they formed the regiment and, under the leadership of Major McClary, marched all night. At sunrise, they were on parade on Cambridge, Mass., Common, as the history tells us, "spilling for a fight."

The men had traveled 56 miles in 20 hours. Those from Epsom had traveled 75 miles in less than 24 hours. They had run most of the way.

At Bunker Hill, Major McClary and the New Hampshire men fought under Colonel John Stark. They held their positions until their ammunition ran out. The New Hampshire men were the last to leave the battlefield. As they retreated, Major McClary was at the rear holding order.

As they crossed the small neck of land from Charlestown, the major went back to note if the enemy was following. His men advised him not to, but Major McClary said, "The ball is not yet cast that will kill me!"

At that moment, a shot came from one of the British ships in the harbor. The bullet glanced off a buttonwood tree and passed through the major's abdomen. The written account of the day says that he threw his hands above his head, leaped into the air, and fell face down upon the ground, dead.

Major Andrew McClary from Epsom was the highest-ranking American officer killed at Bunker Hill. It was also said of him that he was the handsomest man killed that day, as well.

He was buried in Medford, Mass. There is no monument to mark the spot. ❧

Commodore Nutt

P.T. BARNUM'S SMALLEST man was only twenty-five inches high, but he was perfectly proportioned.

His name was *Commodore Nutt,* and he came from Manchester.

There is a turn off South Willow Street in Manchester that leads down to Nutt Pond. It is called Nutt Pond because before the Civil War it was part of a 400-acre farm belonging to a Revolutionary War veteran named Major Rodnia Nutt.

Farmer Nutt had two sons by his first wife; the older son was named after himself, *Rodnia.* The younger son was named *George Washington Morrison Nutt.* Both boys were dwarfs. Both parents were normal-sized, however.

In the mid-1800s, Manchester also had a impresario who traveled around the area providing talent at fairs and firemen's musters and opera houses. His name was *Willie Walker*—not *Willie Wonka*—and he knew a good thing when he saw it.

Willie Walker coached the two young men in singing and dancing, and pretty soon they had an act that was a smash all over New England.

Well, word got through to the greatest showman in America, Phineas T.Barnum, who also produced shows and was the owner of the greatest oddities museum in New York City. He sent an agent to Manchester to hire this perfectly proportioned man who was even smaller than General Tom Thumb.

Barnum claims to have given George Washington Morrison Nutt the title *Commodore* to contrast with the title of *General* he had given Tom Thumb, but it appears that the title was used by impresario Walker. P.T. Barnum, it must be said, was not known for his honesty.

Commodore Nutt was a great sensation in New York, and Barnum even had Tom Thumb return from a road trip to appear with the new little person. And, by the way, the Commodore's brother, Rodnia, was also exhibited, although he was a full head taller than his brother.

About this time another little person entered the scene, the stunningly beautiful Lavinia Warren.

She was the smallest woman in the world, and Barnum decided there was great publicity in having her marry Tom Thumb.

The problem was that Commodore Nutt was madly in love with her, too. And, in fact, Thumb and Nutt came to fisticuffs over her. But Commodore Nutt was only 15 years old. He, however, was not inexperienced. Seems there were many women who fancied him.

But, it seems, Lavinia received a diamond-and-ruby ring from an admirer. It was, however, too big for her finger and she gave it to the Commodore.

The Commodore treated the ring as an engagement and was broken-hearted when Lavinia chose the older, more experienced (and one must also allow, fatter) General Thumb.

The Commodore was best man. He, however, wore the ring from Lavinia to his dying day.

Commodore Nutt went on to become internationally famous. He met with President Lincoln even.

But he drank and caroused. He married a normal-sized woman. He was even arrested for operating a bawdy house.

He died in 1881 of dissipation and "Bright's Disease," an incurable kidney ailment. He was only 33. ❧

Stephen Parker, friend of George Washington

IT WAS 1776. Stephen Parker was plowing his field on City Hill in what is now Nelson, when a neighbor rushed across the field to tell him that British troops were advancing on our troops at Charlestown, Mass.

Parker unhitched his horse, left his plow in the furrow in the field, and rode off.

It would be eight years before he got home.

At Bunker Hill Stephen Parker was hit with a musket ball. The shot went in his cheek and out his mouth. He lost teeth and carried a terrible scar the rest of his life.

For his valiancy, he was made a captain. He fought with George Washington's army in New Jersey and was with him when he crossed the Delaware on Christmas Day. At Valley Forge, he became General Washington's personal guard and protector. To the end of his life, the Father of our Country would salute whenever he met Stephen Parker and call him by name.

In December of 1799, Stephen Parker was again home in his field when, again, a man rode up and said, "General Washington is dead."

The *Nelson Town History* tells us that the old captain took out his blue handkerchief having on it the stars and stripes, wiped his eyes, stuck his ax into a log and went to his house to sit by the fire. He did not speak again that day.

On the Fourth of July in 1814, Stephen Parker hoed corn all morning. At noon, as was his practice every Fourth of July, he took his musket and fired it 14 times, once for every state in the union and once for General Washington.

He then walked to his home where, on the birthday of his nation, he died. ❧

Two-Gun Perkins

IN MID-SEPTEMBER OF 1859, a firemen's muster was held here in Manchester.

Two thousand firemen poured into the city that weekend from all over New England. Most slept in tents set up on Merrimack Common.

That year there was lots of money because the mills were doing so well, and the city had dozens of saloons.

And, that weekend there was gambling. Dice games and card games, horse races and wrestling matches were happening all over the city. Professional gamblers had come up from Lowell and Boston and rented rooms for their businesses.

The night before the muster the saloons were busy. In the Underhill Saloon, the men from the Charlestown, Mass. Fire Company were drinking and gambling with some of the out-of-town pros.

A fireman named Hepburn went to cash in his chips from the faro table and was given a counterfeit five-dollar bank note. Hepburn said nothing, but later went back to the table, ordered five dollars worth of chips and tried to pay for them with the same bank note.

The dealer, an old-time prize fighter named Sullivan, refused to honor the note. Sullivan was not a man to mess with. Sullivan ordered him out of the saloon. Hepburn refused. Sullivan slammed him in the face.

A brawl ensued.

Other firemen from outside on the street joined the melee. The mob destroyed the saloon, trounced all the gamblers and stole all the liquor from behind the bar. They then poured out onto the street and proceeded to the next saloon, an establishment called the Elm House. Here they trashed the place and again stole all the liquor.

By this time, the mob had grown to a couple hundred men.

Next was a saloon and gambling hall operated by a man named Sam Perkins. They totally demolished his place, including all the furniture and glass and, of course, stole all his liquor.

Then it was the Roby Saloon on Elm Street between Spring and Water streets, where the mob discovered one of the gamblers who had been working at the Underhill Saloon where it all started. The man had escaped then and so the mob went after him again. But they were drunk, and he was scared. He outran them and got away. This put the mob in an even uglier mood, and they took it out on the Roby Saloon and its owners.

By this time, other mobs were wrecking other saloons in the city. The American house up on Manchester Street was the headquarters of the gamblers from Boston and that establishment and its occupants suffered mightily from the drunken mob.

The newspaper accounts of the day said that 300 gallons of liquor were destroyed by the mob. Later it was noted that no one saw any destruction of the liquor other than it passing through the kidneys of the rioters.

The police were nowhere to be seen. The day before, the mayor, E.W. Harrington, had told his friends that if there was any trouble, it would be impossible to stop it. So the cops were hiding.

The mob, now grown to half a thousand, approached Washington House. Washington House was owned by a man named Nathaniel Perkins, and the day before, he had gone to the mayor and been deputized as a city policeman. Perkins saw the mob coming and went outside. There on the doorstep of the Washington House he stood, with a pistol in each hand. As the mob approached he calmly said, "Gentlemen," he said, "gentlemen, this place is closed to the public. I'll kill any man who attempts to come in this door . . . or he'll kill me."

The mob quieted down. There was a long pause. And then the firemen dispersed.

There was no more trouble that weekend.

And from that time on, the owner and proprietor of the Washington House in Manchester was known all over New England as "Two-Gun Perkins." ⬥

Franklin Pierce

GEORGE GEERS PHOTOGRAPH

PIERCE HOMESTEAD

The Pierce Homestead was built in 1804 by Benjamin Pierce, a general in the American Revolution, twice governor of New Hampshire (1827-28, 1829-30), and father of Franklin Pierce, the 14th President of the United States (1853-57). Franklin Pierce was born in Hillsboro November 23, 1804 and the family occupied this dwelling shortly thereafter.

The Franklin Pierce Homestead

THE FRANKLIN PIERCE Homestead is in Hillsboro. It is the place where our 14th president was born and spent his boyhood. Now I'll probably get in trouble by saying this, but it seems, every survey they do among historians, Franklin Pierce comes out on the bottom. New Hampshire's president has the reputation for being our worst president to date.

Franklin was born here in 1804. His daddy was Benjamin Franklin, who was to become governor of the state. The house was always filled with people of opinion and power.

Young Franklin grew up pampered by his mother and a little in awe of his dad.

He was a good student . . . went to primary school over in Hancock. He was a bit of a mama's boy, it seems, because one late afternoon he got homesick and walked back to Hillsboro. His dad was not amused and turned him right around and made him walk all the way back in the dark. He was real tired in class the next day.

Young Franklin went off to Bowdoin College in Maine where he was a classmate and best friends with the writer Nathaniel Hawthorne. These two guys really liked each other a lot. Later, Hawthorne was to write Franklin Pierce's biography. Pierce was a great student at Bowdoin, by the way, and graduated third in his class, the class of 1824.

If you research Franklin Pierce, you'll find two things mentioned over and over again. The first is that he was handsome. The young ladies swooned when they saw him. He was delicate and boyish. The other thing that is always mentioned is his drinking. He apparently appeared drunk a lot.

This was maybe because, unlike his dad, Franklin really had no stomach for politics. But his father's name was golden in New Hampshire. And Franklin Pierce served five terms in the U.S. House of Representatives and then, at the age of 37, was elected to the U.S. Senate.

But his wife hated politics. She was Jane Appleton, a beautiful woman . . . but fragile. The couple had three children. Franklin Jr. lived only three days. The second son, Franky, died of typhus. The third son was named after his grandfather, Benjamin.

Due, among other reasons, to Jane's fragile mental health, Franklin Pierce resigned from the U.S. Senate after four years and went back to practicing law in Concord.

But then, in 1852, a couple important things happened . . . Daniel Webster died . . . and Henry Clay died. These were the two great leaders of the Whig Party. Without them the party was rudderless. As a result, they nominated General Winfield Scott to be their candidate for the presidency.

Scott was known to be vainglorious and a windbag.

The Democrats chose Franklin Pierce as their candidate because he was not well known and because he looked good. He also was sympathetic to the South and would not make waves regarding slavery.

Pierce won in a landslide, 254 electoral votes to Scotts' 43 electoral votes. It was a triumph, but it was short-lived. Weeks before the inauguration in Washington D.C., the train Franklin, Jane and her son Benny were riding left the tracks and crashed.

Benny was killed. Jane said it was God punishing them for their hubris. She never recovered. Nor did Franklin Pierce himself. Their stay in Washington was drab and depressing.

During his term, Franklin Pierce rigidly enforced the fugitive slave law and signed the Kansas-Nebraska Act which was the event most historians feel made the Civil War inevitable.

Pierce returned home to Concord after his term and lived out his life in obscurity. He died in 1869 at the age of 65. ❧

General John Porter

DURING THE CIVIL War, Union General John Pope commanded the Army of Virginia and he was out to get Stonewall Jackson.

Pope hated Confederates and, especially, Jackson, and on August 28, 1862, he felt he finally had him. That day General Jackson had attacked a Union brigade to begin what would be called "The Second Battle of Bull Run."

Pope was imperious and egotistical. He was not liked by his men. He was not liked by, nor did he like, General McClellan, the head of the Union forces.

Pope sent for more troops. General McClellan responded by sending his Fifth Corps. The Fifth was under the command of General Fitz-John Porter; twelve thousand troops in all.

At the time, General Porter was regarded as, perhaps, the finest soldier in the Army of the Potomac. He was brave, smart and loyal. He was second in command only to McClellan.

General Porter and his corps set off immediately for the battle.

In the meantime, Confederates were moving up men, too. Twenty thousand men were also marching to join with Stonewall Jackson's troops.

Word was sent to General Pope that Longstreet was on the move. Pope ignored the information.

General Porter was ordered to attack the center of Stonewall Jackson's position; the center was a railroad cut. Porter's troops went at it and almost took it. But in the end the Confederates prevailed.

Then the 25,000 Confederates, whom Pope had been warned of, attacked Pope's flank.

General Porter and his men retreated to a stand on Henry House Hill. This saved the Army of Virginia from total destruction.

But the Second Battle of Bull Run was a total rout and a huge embarrassment for the Union Army.

They needed a scapegoat, and it wasn't going to be General Pope. What better than to blame the humiliation on General McClellan's second in command, General Fitz-John Porter. And so it was done.

He was charged with failing to follow a direct order to re-attack Jackson's center.

That his troops had been flanked by Longstreet, had been attacked and had fought valiantly and had, in the end, saved the Army from total capitulation was no excuse.

Also at the time there was a congressional organization called The Committee on the Conduct of the War. These were Radical Republicans who supported only abolitionist generals and attacked conservative ones, no matter what their competence. They were firmly against General Porter.

And so the fix was in. The Army Court Martial Panel was packed with enemies of McClellan and General Fitz-John Porter was cashiered out of the Army, stripped of his pension and forbidden ever to run for public office.

Total humiliation.

And so it remained for 22 years.

But there were those who were witness to the events who knew what a travesty the proceedings had been . . . people who knew and loved the general.

And finally, in 1886, a military board was convened and, after hearing dozens of witnesses, voted unanimously to exonerate the general of all charges.

Ergo, his statue in Haven park, Portsmouth. ❧

Rybo

WHEN I WAS growing up, my father and my uncles and their friends always had Rybo Chase stories. Rybo was a guy who did stuff and was always in trouble.

My Uncle Glen used to tell about Rybo's greatest prank. Sometime in the 1920s, seems Rybo set off a bunch of fireworks from the bandstand on the Milford Town Common. Set the rockets off horizontally and broke a dozen or so windows around The Oval. The merchants weren't all that pleased, but Rybo's contemporaries told the story over and over again for years.

Rybo used to drink and, when he did, he would announce that when he died he wanted to be buried on the town common with just his head sticking up as a comfort station for dogs.

If there was a prank or a practical joke, the first person people went looking for was Rybo.

Well, Rybo died. And my dad said that at his funeral there was a teriffic turn out. Seems he died in the winter and they put the body in the vault out at Riverside Cemetery. See, there was a false grave over the vault so there could be a completion to the services with the body being lowered with the mourners standing around. The actual interment would be in the spring when the ground was thawed.

Anyhow, the cortege came into the cemetery and the coffin was placed in the lowering straps above the vault. The final words were said over the body and then the pins were pulled and the coffin slowly began its descent into the vault.

Well, here is where it happened.

Dad said the mechanism got hung up and only one side of the casket went down and, of course, it twisted and Rybo fell against the top and it came open.

And the widow swooned, and everyone gasped.

But, at the same time, there were great huge smiles amid the tears.

Rybo would have loved it. ❧

Caleb Stark

SHE WEIGHED 315 pounds.

Her husband, Caleb Page, loved her, not in spite of her girth and size but rather because of it.

She had been the Widow Carlton when he asked her to marry him. Caleb Page liked everything big.

He married his second wife in 1740—two years after his first wife Ruth had died and three years after their daughter Elizabeth had been born.

Caleb Page was a rich man. Under his bed were gold guineas and silver crowns and dollars and jewelry. Caleb Page owned hundreds of acres at his home in Atkinson.

In 1750, Caleb Page sold out and moved his wife and daughter out to the frontier of New Hampshire—to Starktown.

Before he left he put his estate up for sale. His asking price: the weight of his wife in silver dollars. That land is today where the Atkinson Academy sits and all the land extending out from it to the east, west, south and north for about a mile.

He found a buyer and went to the wilderness where he built a fort.

Starktown was a very small place then, about a hundred people. But Elizabeth Page was known for miles around for her independence and her spirit and ability, but mostly for her fair looks.

So there you have it, a small town with a fabulously rich man, a 300-pound wife and a beautiful daughter. The family was well-known and Elizabeth had many suitors. But only one young man found favor with the maiden. He was an explorer who had gone out to the Connecticut River Valley where he had been captured by Indians and taken from there to Canada where he was ransomed by the French.

But on the twentieth of February in 1758, the young man arrived back home where he rode at once to the home of Elizabeth Page. She burst from the door and ran to him and he, without dismounting, said, "If you are ever to become my wife, Molly, you will have to come with me now."

And so, Elizabeth (whose nickname was, of course, "Molly") mounted the horse behind her lover and went off. The young man was, of course, John Stark who was to be a hero of Bunker Hill and the man who was to turn the course of the American Revolution at the Battle of Bennington.

Before the battle, General Stark told his troops, "Yonder are the British and they are ours boys, or Molly Stark sleeps a widow tonight." The battle was a great victory for the Americans. Not incidentally, John Stark also gave the state of New Hampshire its motto: "Live Free or Die."

During the Revolution, General Stark gave his residence as Starktown and Molly lived in her father's house during that time. Their first son was born there and named after his grandfather, "Caleb," and the son continued to live with his grandfather even after the war when his father took the rest of the family to a home in Manchester.

On the death of his grandfather, the younger Caleb became the chief beneficiary of his estate. He died a rich man.

Molly's 300-pound stepmother expired soon after their move to Starktown.

And Starktown changed its name . . . to Dunbarton. And Molly's house still stands. ❧

Herman Straw

IN THE EARLY days of the Amoskeag Mills, Manchester was an example to the world for the treatment of workers.

The wages were good for the time, and the company took care of everything . . . cradle to grave. There were parks and ball fields and clubs and lectures provided by the company as well as places for the workers to live.

Many loved the company. When Edwin Jones went to England in 1870, he visited Manchester, England, and noted that the workers there wore wooden shoes because they could not afford leather ones.

He noted that even the lowest laborer in the Manchester Mills of New Hampshire was well-fed and clothed. Later, of course, the company would fall into bad times and the great social experiment would be over. But at first, Manchester, New Hampshire, was a showplace for the world.

Ezekiel Straw was one of the company agents in the mid-1800s, and he was the man who ran the mill. And he was highly thought of. His son, Herman Straw, took over the reigns of the company from his dad and Herman was even more respected.

There are hundreds of stories about Herman Straw. He was a distant sort of person. No one ever called him by his first name. Even his close friends, and he had many, called him Mr. Straw.

He seemed aloof and formal but he truly loved his job and more importantly, his workers. A story here is instructive.

Seems one of his boyhood friends had been a mechanic at Amoskeag and had given the company years of service but had failed in his health. The man applied for an early retirement from the company with a pension and was granted that.

But nothing had been said about the apartment in the tenement where he lived. The matter was brought to the attention of Herman Straw.

Mr. Straw leaned back in his chair and thought for a minute. Then he said, "Charles and I were boys together. He had a double runner. My father would never let me have one. I used to go over to my friend's house evenings and we would slide. And he would also loan it to me.

"My father never knew of it and I have always felt that Charlie shared some of the things in life that were denied to me. You may tell him that he may have that tenement for life," he said.

"Or as long as I am head of this outfit."

That is just one story about Herman Straw. There are many more and all tell of a wonderful man. ❧

Tommy Wiggins

THERE ISN'T MUCH wiggle room in any kind of authority nowadays. In the bigger corporations, in order to fire someone, you first have to build a paper trail, or you may find yourself in court.

Judges now have mandatory sentencing. Teachers are afraid to discipline students. In other words, due to the litigious nature of a lot of people nowadays, a great deal of common sense has gone out of the world.

Back when I was a young man, there was a police officer on the Milford force whom everyone respected. When Officer Chickie Ethridge said something to you, you paid attention (because the guy was fair and smart and something that is always rare, he had wisdom).

Tommy Wiggins was home on leave from the U.S. Navy. His ship was in port in New York Harbor, and Tom and a friend of his had come to New Hampshire for some R-and-R.

The time was 1960 or '61. (And yes, by the way, Tommy Wiggins is a direct male descendant of *the* Thomas Wiggins, one of the original settlers of New Hampshire. I just say this because I'm just sure someone is going to email me and ask. So, yes.)

Anyhow, back to the story: Tom and his buddy were out partying. Tom was driving a car, but his license had expired. That wasn't a problem back then because, if you were in the service, you didn't have to update your automobile license as long as you had the old one and proof that you were in the service. Tom had both those things.

So, like I say, it's the early '60s and the guys have been to a couple of parties in New Boston and other places, and it is now one in the morning. They are driving from Milford toward Mont Vernon and, right at the old Hartson's Mill, the blue gum machine light goes on behind them. Cops.

Tommy pulls over and Officer Chickie Ethridge comes up and shines his light in at the two sailors.

"Hi, Tommy."

"Hi, Chickie."

"You boys been drinking?"

"Yeah, we had a couple, I guess."

"Lets see your license . . . hmm, this is expired, Tommy."

So Tommy tells him about the fact he doesn't need a current license and Chickie agrees he's right.

Now Officer Ethridge knows that the guys should not be driving and he has the power to make their lives hell if chooses. Late back from leave is not fun. So he reaches into Tommy's car and takes the keys from the ignition.

"Tommy," he says, "when you find these keys, you can drive home." And he throws them over the car and way up in the pucker brush up from the road.

Tommy told me that the sun had been up three hours before they finally found the keys. By that time, both sailors were dog tired, so cold they were shivering, very chagrined . . . and stone sober. ❧

Henry Wilson

JEREMIAH JONES COLBATH knew poverty.

Years later, when he was a success, he said, "I know what it is to ask a mother for bread when she has none to give."

Jeremiah Jones Colbath was born in Farmington in 1812. He was the first of eight children.

His father, Winthrope Colbath, was a drunk and a brute who worked in a sawmill. His mother, Abigail, was a domestic who cleaned the homes of the more prominent citizens of the town. Among those citizens was the sister of Governor Levi Woodbury, Mrs. Anstress Eastman.

The story is Mrs. Eastman caught Jeremiah fighting with another child in the street and broke the fight up. She discovered that he was the son of her housekeeper and invited the lad home and took an interest in him.

Jeremiah Colbath went to school until he was 10. But on his 10th birthday his dad sold him to a neighbor, William Knight.

True. It was, in fact, common practice in the 19th century. Farmers needed labor and poor people needed to feed their children. So, often children were placed as indentured servants. When they became adults, of course, they were released.

And so it was with Jeremiah Colbath.

His father's contract with farmer Knight required a month's schooling each year, but it was on a catch-as-catch-can basis. However, Jeremiah Colbath was able to borrow books from Mrs. Eastman and when he visited his mother she would have a copy of the *Dover Gazette* borrowed from one of the homes she cleaned.

Farmer Knight was a deeply religious man . . . and a skinflint. He required church-going and hard work. Jeremiah took after his mother and was diligent. But he hated his father.

Of the eight children his parents had, three died in childhood from the effects of poverty. At 19, in reaction to his father's drunkenness, Jeremiah Colbath took an oath of temperance. In his entire life he was never to drink alcohol.

· He also espoused emancipation and women's rights.

When Jeremiah Colbath turned 21, farmer Knight gave him his freedom and, as the contract required, some sheep and oxen which the young man promptly sold for $84. He then petitioned the State of New Hampshire to change his name. It was the final revenge on his father.

Henceforth, Jeremiah Jones Colbath would be called Henry Wilson. It is not known why he chose this name. Speculation is that it was because of a General James Wilson whom he admired, but the young man never explained his choice.

He went to Natick, Massachusetts, where he apprenticed as a cobbler, became successful and soon owned factories.

On a trip to Washington D.C., he saw the slave markets within sight of the Capitol building itself. It was a seminal moment.

Henry Wilson returned to Massachusetts and ran for Congress. He was ever the radical and, during his political career, he identified himself with many of the new parties. He ran as a Whig and as a No-Nothing; as a Free Soiler and, finally, as a Republican.

After the Civil War, he was disappointed in the government of Andrew Johnson. He was among the first to call for his impeachment. And, finally, when Ulysses Grant ran for his second term, Henry Wilson was elected his vice president. In 1875, Henry Wilson suffered a stroke on the floor of the House of Representatives. He was carried to the Vice President's Room just off the chamber, where there was a small bed. A couple of days later, still there in the chamber room, he died. He was 63.

And that's the story of the only person from the state of New Hampshire ever to become vice president of the United States. ❧

THE WETHERBEES

Ira Wetherbee

ON ROUTE 63, leading into the town of Chesterfield, is a small en-
closed area with a stone that certainly attracted my interest the first
time I saw it.

It reads, Joab Wetherbee.

Wetherbee, I note, is spelled the way my family spells it. So I
looked it up in our genealogy and yes, Joab is a distant relative.

He was born in Lunenburg, Mass., in 1759. He was married to
Abigail Houghton from Leominster. The couple migrated to Chesterfield, where they owned a farm.

They had a son, Ira. His name is also on the gravestone. And it is
Ira who is the most interesting of the bunch. Ira was, to all intents
and purposes, a scoundrel.

He was a gambler known in Keene and Brattleboro for being
deeply in debt. He was also said to have been very handsome, tall
and thin, and was an expert horseman. He also had a nice disposition
and was courteous to ladies.

Unfortunately, he had a character flaw. It all stemmed, the town
history tells us, from his school days. Seems he had a dispute with
the local schoolteacher. The teacher, it is said, punished him severely.
The upshot was that the next day the schoolhouse burned down.

Over the next few years some of the barns and outbuildings of his
father's farm also burned and so did some other local buildings.

Because of his gambling debts, Ira left town and returned only for visits to his dad and mom once in awhile. As much of a scoundrel as he was, he was well-liked. It was said that he always took up for the weaker side.

In 1849, Ira Wetherbee left Chesterfield and New Hampshire for good; went to California and the Gold Rush. He died out there and is presumed buried there, although no one seems to know where. ❧

Indiana Burns

LIFE WAS HARD in the 18th century.

Life was particularly hard in New England.

Farming here was mostly pulling up rocks. And most people who lived in New England then were farmers.

But word was that in the west the soil was fertile and easy to plow . . . and cheap.

Joseph Burns, his wife Nancy, and their five children lived out on the family farm on the Brookline Road in Milford. Joseph's grandfather had been one of the original citizens of Milford. There is a plaque at the place he settled.

It's called Burns rock. You can see it to this day.

But Joseph wanted more for his family than the rock-scrabble farm, and he had saved and scrimped and signed on to a wagon train that was moving west in April of 1799.

Joseph's family also had grief. Two years before, their youngest child, 2 1/2-half-year-old Ira, had died of diphtheria. All the more reason to move west. It would be a new start.

However, just before the family was to leave, Nancy announced she was pregnant again.

What to do? The trip would be arduous. Nancy would, no doubt, be all right.

But what if she lost the child?

It was decided that they would not travel with the wagon train but rather wait until the baby was born, and then go with another group.

And so it was that Joseph and Nancy Burns stayed in Milford that year and a fine, healthy baby girl was born who was the favorite of the family.

Joseph and Nancy never went west. The closest they ever came was to name their daughter Indiana Burns, for the place they had been bound for.

Indiana Burns, by the way, was my great, great grandmother. ◆

Militia training day

BACK IN THE early days of Brookline, the biggest event of the year was always the militia training day.

Militia training was held every May on the parade ground. There was marching and fife and drum corps and food and games . . . in other words, a sort of fair.

In the Brookline town history, there is a recount of a militia day held back in the 1840s.

On that day, the members of the local militia assembled in the local tavern to get organized . . . but, because it was a tavern, that organization was not very organized. In fact, the men were drunk by the time Captain Artemas Wright told the drummer boy to roll the drum to assemble the men. The line they formed, the history tells us, undulated and waved back and forth like a lose rope swayed by the wind.

Obeying the captain's commands, the men managed to "right face" and "size up" and "front face." They were making a vigorous effort to "right dress" when one of the members of the militia, a distant relative of mine, one "Timothy Wetherbee" stepped out of line.

Now, Tim Wetherbee was a small man "of diminutive height" is what the town history says of him. Anyhow, little Tim walks up to this guy who is leaning against a porch of one of the houses. The guy is smirking. So Tim punches him right in the nose (hey, what can I tell you? This is all in the town history.) Well, the two men are soon rolling around on the ground punching and kicking and swearing and scratching until the bystanders pull them apart.

Little Tim Wetherbee springs right back in line with his musket.

"Wetherbee," the captain says, "you are fined 25 cents!"

"I don't give a damn, sir," says Tim. "I'll pay it, sir!" says he. "But I want you to distinctly understand, sir, that there can't no damned Massachusetts' man come over here and grin at this company when it's on parade, sir!"

Captain Wright then gave the order, and the men marched away. ☙

Father sees his first naked lady

IN 1915, MY dad was 9 years old and lived on the corner of Clinton and Nashua streets in Milford.

Down the street lived the Colby family. I remember Charlie Colby quite well. They burned wood, I remember, and were always having chimney fires.

Anyhow, that's beside the point.

What is to the point is that Charlie had a maiden aunt living with the family who had a bedroom on the first floor in the back of the house.

Well, my dad and his best friend, "Linky" Gilson, were roaming around the neighborhood one evening, and they snuck up to Miss Colby's room and peeked into the window.

See, it was summertime, and Miss Colby had the window up about six inches to allow the wind to blow in. She had pulled the shade just down to the bottom of the window and no farther so it wouldn't blow.

Well, Dad and Linky couldn't believe their luck. Miss Colby was getting ready for bed and they witnessed her whole ritual—and back in those days, they tell me, there was quite a ritual.

Well, of course, Dad and Linky came back the next night and the next . . . and the next.

Then one night, Linky couldn't stand it any more and waited until Miss Colby was totally naked and then he reached into the room and took hold of the shade and pulled it down and let it go.

Well, up it went. And Linky, knowing what he was about to do, was nowhere to be seen. But my dad was right there in the window paralyzed by the blood-curdling scream Miss Colby was directing at him.

Well, Dad had a talk with his dad later that night right after a contingent of the Colby family had left their home.

Dad and Linky remained best friends to the end of their lives and, every time they went hunting, they'd tell that story again. I heard it dozens of times.

You know, if that story happened nowadays, nobody would laugh. ❧

Peterborough theater days

THE PETERBOROUGH PLAYERS is one of the oldest professional summer theatres in the nation. It dates from 1933 and, in 1957, I was an apprentice here. Those are the kids that come and do all the chores around a theatre and learn to act and they're in some of the plays. And that year there was an apprentice show we did, "Cradle Song," which is a weepy tear-jerker about this foundling that the nuns take into this place in Spain.

They raise her in the convent. Her name is Theresa; she lives there, and then at the end of the play she goes away. She marries an American, they get on a boat and sail for America and she's never seen again by any of the nuns in the convent who were all kind of like surrogate mothers to her.

In the end of the play there were, of course, handkerchiefs all out and everyone was weeping. I was cast in this play as the kindly old doctor, the freethinker. And at the end of the play, they're coming to take Theresa away from the convent forever. The bags are all there and the nuns are around and they're trying to cry and the audience is crying. To make small talk, one of the nuns says to the doctor, who was me, "How old are you, Doctor?" And I say, "I'm eighty-six." And she says, "Well, that's remarkable." And I say, "It's probably because I'm preserved in sanctity like a fly in thick syrup."

Well, it came the night for the performance, the only performance, the big deal for the whole year, and the play went swimmingly. I mean people were weeping. You could hear them in the audience just sobbing uncontrollably. And I came on stage to take Theresa away forever and the nun turned to me and said, to make small talk, "How old are you, Doctor?" And I said, "I'm eighty-six," and she said, "Why you would never know it." I said, "It's probably because I'm preserved in syrup."

I remember Bill Armstrong who was an usher ran up the aisle howling, just laughing hysterically and out into the courtyard. You could here him going hee-hee-hee-hee and, of course, the audience picked up on it and they laughed and they laughed and they laughed.

The nuns on stage were looking at me saying things that nuns would never say. Luckily it was right at the end of the season and the people went home after the play, and I never saw most of them again. ◆

Dr. Webber and the dog

YOU ARE NOT out of this life even after you are dead sometimes.

Sometimes things happen after the end which could be the things people remember the most. For instance, Dr. Webber.

Dr. Frederick Webber was the physician for my family over in Milford back in the 1940s. (I think his name was Frederick.) He had his practice down on South Street in the old Pillsbury House on the east side of the street.

Dr. Webber also had a cottage on Heads Pond in Hooksett that we used to go to now and then, when I was a kid. I remember we ate lobster at a big wooden table there.

Anyhow, about 1948 or so, Dr Webber died and his funeral was held at the old Tucker funeral home on High Street, just up the hill above his office.

It was summer and it was hot. All the doors of the old fin de siecle house were open and there was cross ventilation, but still people were fanning themselves with their printed eulogies as they sat waiting for the service to begin.

Dr. Webber was laid out amidst the flowers and, being a beloved man, there were many tears that day. Occasionally, someone would blow his nose.

The flowers smelled beautiful.

What happened next has been told and retold in my family for years:

As the organ played, a tiny "pit-a-pat" sound was heard and right down the middle of the aisle came a small dog with a turned-up tail. To this day, I don't know whose dog it was.

Tick-tick-tick-tick-tick it went right up to the bier, sniffed and lifted its leg. And there in the sunshine of a summer's day, that sweet little dog peed on the flowers, turned, and "tick-tick-tick-tick-tick" walked back up the center aisle and out of the building.

The minister then arrived and gave the service . . .

. . . and wondered why the entire congregation was smiling. ◈

Sometimes

ON A FALL morning in 1969 in Milford, my brother, Carl, and his wife Linda opened a restaurant.

It was unlike any restaurant opening you ever heard of. Here's the story:

Seems Avery Johnson had purchased the old train depot on South Street. Avery was a wealthy guy with a Ph.D. in engineering from MIT. He was very bright and was one of the great icons of the Hippie Generation. He was always doing stuff like lending one of his properties to some flower people. Oh, I didn't mention, my brother, Carl, and his wife were hippies.

Well, Avery had bought the old depot and wasn't doing anything with it. Enter Carl and Linda: "Let's open a restaurant there." Of course, they didn't have any capital, but they had a location and Avery would defer the rent. So, why not?

So, Carl and Linda and Avery and their friends cleaned up the place. It had never been a restaurant, but it had been a neighborhood store with an apartment in the back, so there was a small kitchen and some of the coolers left from the old store. It cost them $40 to register the business with the state and another few dollars for postage for postcards, which they sent out. All in all, less than a $100 and they were in business.

Oh, you say, but where are the tables and the flatware and the plates and napkins and cooking utensils and . . . where is the food?

Well, you see, that's what the cards were for.

They sent out invitations which said something on the line of, "Please come to the opening of 'Sometimes.'"

(Oh, I forgot to tell you they decided to call the place "Sometimes" because . . . well, because it would be open sometimes.)

. . . Anyhow, it said, "Please come to the opening of 'Sometimes,' a new restaurant located in the depot on South Street. Unfortunately, we have no tables, no chairs, no silverware, no plates, napkins, cooking pots . . . and no food. Please come and bring any of the above and be charged exorbitantly for your own food!"

Well, of course, it was a great success. On that Sunday morning outside the restaurant there was a line of dozens of people. They were carrying all sorts of stuff wanting to get in and sit at their own tables and eat their own food off their own plates. Everyone was laughing and having a great time and, when the day was done, not only did Carl and Linda have a full restaurant with all the stuff they needed and lots of food, they also had enough left over for a great yard sale to up the cash flow.

"Sometimes" lasted about a year. It closed when Carl and Linda's marriage came to a close. But in that time, they had lots of volunteer chefs who came by and cooked their favorite meals . . . and author Rick Frede did a rave review of the restaurant for *The Boston Globe*.

For a few months after Carl and Linda left, the restaurant became a place that specialized in quiche and was run by a guy, as I recall, by the name of Bob who was also doing primal scream therapy. ✒

Monkey Rock

A DOZEN OR SO years ago, the New Hampshire Highway Department re-paved and widened the road between New Boston and Francestown, Route 33.

In doing so, they uncovered some rocks from some of the embankments. Someone told me that one of these rocks looked something like an ape's head. I went to see it. As I had a video crew with me, I showed it on television.

"This," I said, "is Monkey Rock!"

The day after the program was broadcast, a UPS truck passed and the driver shouted to me, "Monkey Rock!" and put thumbs up.

I heard that the kids on the bus on the way to school also shouted, "Monkey Rock!" as they passed it.

Now, I must say, not everyone was pleased. John Van Skoyik, the news director at Channel 5 in Boston at the time, brought his kids out to see the rock based on my enthusiasm. He said his kids thought it didn't look anything like a monkey! I had wasted his whole day, and he wasn't going to forget it.

Also, there is the matter of where the rock is. It is too close to the highway and, sooner or later, will have to be removed because it obviously is a traffic hazard.

But it has been here a dozen years now and a whole generation has grown up with it. And the moss has grown over it, so now it looks as if it has always been here. I for one don't think it should ever be moved.

Monkey Rock forever! ❧

Ironic Fritz

GEORGE GEERS PHOTOGRAPH

I AM STANDING at the counter at Dunkin' Donuts and I say, "I'd like a coffee . . . ah, an iced coffee."

And the woman behind the counter says, "Say iced first because I am not a mind-reader."

"Sorry," I say. "And milk, ah, skim milk."

And she says, "Well, I almost put plain milk into the cup. Say skim milk if you want it."

"And a regular hot coffee with just cream."

"What size?"

"Ah, small, I guess."

"I have to know the size," she says.

"I know," I say.

"You look like that guy on television," she says.

"I get that a lot," I say.

" You sound like him, too."

"Yeah, I know."

"He's knowledgeable, though," she says.

I'm at the check-out counter at Ames in Concord buying a t-shirt and a lady in front of me turns and says, "Oh," she says, "You're Fritz Wetherbee. I watch you all the time."

"Thanks," I say.

She leaves and the kid behind the counter is looking at me. "You on TV?" he asks.

"Yeah," I say.

He's looking at me. He hasn't a clue.

"Is it a comedy?" he asks.

So I am in Hanover one winter evening drinking dinner with a lady friend and, as we are leaving the restaurant to take a brisk walk, Sister Sledge is playing the rock classic, "We Are Family," which stays in my head as we start up the sidewalk.

I am goofy and in full "horses'-posterior" mode and singing at the top of my lungs. "We are family, all my sisters and me. We are family . . . "

I am also dancing but there is no one on the street 'cause it's cold and late, when suddenly some guy appears coming toward us and he walks over and says, "Please, please, not so loud! And, for gosh sakes, be a little conservative. This is Hanover, after all, be a little demure."

Well, I am shocked and don't know what to say.

"By the way," he says, "I watch you all the time; good job," he says. ❧